Praise for *Feedback (and Other Dirty Words)*

"Feedback can be tough to give (and receive!) but is so core to how we drive performance and improve as humans. This book offers practical frameworks and tools to consider as you leverage feedback to build relationships and improve results!"
—**Jesse Schlueter, Vice President of Learning and Leadership, Nordstrom**

"An enjoyable and compelling read, this book shows leaders how to set the tone for the growth mindset to flourish. Packed with tips, it shows readers an easier path to hearing how they are doing, sharing what they see in others, and inspiring everyone to thrive."
—**Elizabeth Hall, Vice President, Employee Experience, Cambia Health Solutions**

"The way we work is changing. The traditional top-down hierarchal approach to management has been replaced by a collaborative work environment where employees thrive on real-time, continuous feedback from managers. In *Feedback (and Other Dirty Words)*, Chandler and Grealish offer business leaders an informative and easy-to-follow guide for transforming their work culture into one where employees no longer fear feedback but flourish with it."
—**Derek Irvine, Senior Vice President, Client Stra~~t~~ Workhuman**

"Like it or probably not, people don't ~~...~~ ~~...~~ deliver feedback without closin~~g~~ ~~...~~ ~~...~~ ealish give the tools and methods fo~~...~~ ~~...~~. Not only will *Feedback (and Other Dirty V~~...~~* ~~...~~ur next performance conversation, it can transfor~~...~~ ~~...~~ culture to be more agile and enjoyable."
—**Marcia Reynolds, PsyD, Past President, ~~...~~ernational Coach Federation, and author of *The Discomfort Zone***

"This quick read highlights real benefits that can follow strong feedback practices while simultaneously helping to remove the stigma associated with giving and receiving feedback—important topics for leaders."
—**Roy Bivens, author of *Experiencing Improvement*; Managing Partner, Orion Advisory; and CEO, Diamond Orthopedic**

"What do successful leaders and organizations have in common? A culture where feedback is welcomed and not feared and trust sits at the center. *Feedback (and other Dirty Words)* shows you how to get there. Both witty and enlightening! Read this . . . you'll be entertained as much as you are informed."
—**Christopher J. Cowan, MEd, FABC, Senior Vice President, Human Resources, Christiana Care Health System**

"At last! A concise, practical, actionable contribution to the sticky topic of feedback. In this breakthrough book, M. Tamra Chandler and Laura Grealish offer layers of useful information and support for changing our existing paradigms about feedback. This book details simple and powerful methods, backed by science, and everyday examples that the reader can relate to. The authors' wealth of experience shows up in this compelling and digestible tool box."
—**Beatrice W. Hansen, MSSW, PCC, Principal, Presence-Based Coaching**

"This very useful book teaches us that feedback is the key to all activities where we interact with others, especially at work. The lessons here show us how to do it simply and well."
—**Peter Cappelli, George W. Taylor Professor of Management and Director, Center for Human Resources, The Wharton School, and Professor of Education, University of Pennsylvania**

"There is no leadership practice more effective than well done feedback to drive high performance through people. It is the equivalent of a leader superpower. Yet very few have mastered it. How could this power shortage be so severe and stubbornly stuck? What will it take to fix it? Read this clever and awesomely helpful book that digs deep to find the science and reasons behind this power failure, to fully appreciate the proven impact of good feedback, and, importantly, to find many useful and practical strategies and tactics for making your own feedback power super."
—**Jeannie Coyle, former Senior Vice President of Human Resources, American Express, and coauthor of *Make Talent Your Business***

"Thoughtful feedback is both a gift and a critical data point along anyone's journey to their own integrity—and the integrity of any organization. If you want to unleash a powerful and priceless resource, immerse yourself in this book and all that it teaches."
—**Luke Timmins, Head of Engineering, Bungie**

FEEDBACK

(and Other Dirty Words)

FEEDBACK

(and Other Dirty Words)

Why We Fear It, How to Fix It

M. TAMRA CHANDLER
with LAURA DOWLING GREALISH

Berrett–Koehler Publishers, Inc.

Berrett-Koehler Publishers, Inc.
1333 Broadway, Suite 1000
Oakland, CA 94612-1921
Tel: (510) 817-2277
Fax: (510) 817-2278
www.bkconnection.com

ORDERING INFORMATION
Quantity sales. Special discounts are available on quantity purchases by corporations, associations, and others. For details, contact the "Special Sales Department" at the Berrett-Koehler address above.
Individual sales. Berrett-Koehler publications are available through most bookstores. They can also be ordered directly from Berrett-Koehler: Tel: (800) 929-2929; Fax: (802) 864-7626; www.bkconnection.com.
Orders for college textbook / course adoption use. Please contact Berrett-Koehler: Tel: (800) 929-2929; Fax: (802) 864-7626.

Distributed to the U.S. trade and internationally by Penguin Random House Publisher Services.

Berrett-Koehler and the BK logo are registered trademarks of Berrett-Koehler Publishers, Inc.

Printed in Canada

Berrett-Koehler books are printed on long-lasting acid-free paper. When it is available, we choose paper that has been manufactured by environmentally responsible processes. These may include using trees grown in sustainable forests, incorporating recycled paper, minimizing chlorine in bleaching, or recycling the energy produced at the paper mill.

Cataloging-in-Publication Data is available from the Library of Congress

Library of Congress Cataloging in Publication Control Number: 2019002818

First Edition
25 24 23 22 21 20 19   10 9 8 7 6 5 4 3 2 1

Set in A Caslon Pro by Westchester Publishing Services.
Text designer: Jordan Wannemacher
Cover designer: Logan Grealish
Illustrations: Ivy Mosier and Logan Grealish

For Martha Marie Chandler,
who never hesitated to share frequent and focused feedback.
Mom, you are greatly missed.

CONTENTS

INTRODUCTION

WE'VE GOT WORK TO DO

I F YOU ASK MEMBERS of any group of people—multinational corporations, sports teams, "mom and pop" businesses, rock bands, nonprofit boards, knitting clubs, you name it—they're likely to admit that their organization pretty much sucks at feedback. Sure, I've met a few individuals who feel like they navigate the hazardous waters of feedback well, but at an organizational level we're all pretty much adrift.

The depth of our collective angst over feedback has become obvious to me through my work in performance management during the past several years. In 2016, my first book, *How Performance Management Is Killing Performance and What to Do about It*, was published. Applying the concepts from the book, my PeopleFirm team and I work with dozens of organizations ranging from global corporations to private companies to NGOs to reboot their performance management approaches and processes, bringing the outmoded and deeply unpopular traditional approach to performance management into the modern world. While no two solutions we implement are identical, elements of the best designs tend to reoccur.

The most common element centers on enhancing feedback within and across the enterprise. Our best solutions focus on building organizational strength for growth-oriented feedback, not in a traditional manager-to-subordinate framework, but on a human-to-human and team-to-team basis, without regard for rank and title.

Leaders place their organizations' readiness for more of this kind of frequent, open, honest, and helpful feedback at the top of their list of goals. Yet, as soon as we begin to move toward a solution that's dependent on making feedback flow frequently and transparently, we hear the same things: "We're not good at feedback. We're not ready. We lack the skills. We lack the confidence. Our managers are unprepared. Our culture won't support it. People will weaponize it. We don't have the discipline. We just can't do it."

You get the idea.

It's this sadly predictable response that has convinced me that we need to take a collective approach to solving the problem of feedback once and for all. To create organizational cultures that encourage people and teams to thrive, grow, and do their best work in an environment that feels safe, we need to tame this beast. And if it's getting in the way for nearly all of us, then we absolutely must tackle it together. We can build skills and mentally prepare for this transformation, but first we need to understand what's standing in our way and how to get past it. We can do this by aligning to a new definition of feedback and a common set of principles, while adopting easy-to-use models and tools and practicing them every day. Let's put fear in the rearview mirror and head for a place where feedback helps and doesn't hurt—where we all can agree on a new and better concept of what feedback is, then develop a sustainable and workable cure for what's ailing it.

I AM NOT A RELATIONSHIP EXPERT

Spending so much of my time immersed in the world of performance management motivated me to devote my second book to the all-important subject of feedback. After weeks of outlining and brainstorming I worked with my writing partner, Laura Grealish, to put together a spiffy book proposal to send to our publisher. Every book proposal needs to identify the audience you intend to reach and suggest how you expect the book to be marketed. The original pitch to our publisher, Berrett-Koehler, claimed that this book would be for everyone: it could be used by businesses, schools, families, you name it. It seemed like the right idea; after all, feedback is a ubiquitous topic and a universal pain in the butt.

However, once we got the thumbs-up and began writing in earnest, I realized that, while the concepts and tips in this book could be used just about any time two or more people are interacting, the goal really was never to write a book to help people manage their relationships with their mothers, sisters, partners, or teenagers. My true aim was, and remains, helping organizations and the people in them get better, stronger, and more engaged. That's my passion, that's my life, that's what I was put here to do. Suddenly, just a few days into our writing, I told Laura about my revelation, and we agreed that this would definitely be a business book—specifically, one focused on making the world of work a better place through better feedback.

That evening I shared this news with my husband (who also serves as my line editor). He quickly agreed that this was a good idea—almost too quickly.

"You know, this absolutely makes sense," he said. After a pause, he added, "I mean, it's not like you're some kind of relationship expert." Well, he was right, but that stung a bit. Still, there's hope that editing this book helps improve his feedback skills.

I give you this peek behind the creative curtain only to make it clear that this book was written through an organizational lens. It's about people and work and helping each other thrive in that environment. That doesn't mean you can't use these ideas and tips in the rest of your life, of course; if you find it helps you improve communication with your teenager or your spouse, then that's a bonus. But before you apply anything you find in this book to your personal life, remember this important fact: *I am not a relationship expert.* Just ask my husband.

FEEDBACK SHORTCOMINGS, FEEDBACK SUCCESSES

Your business will only rise to the level of your people. This simple truth has been my guiding principle as I've built and sustained environments where people advance rapidly, where they're frequently stretched to their maximum potential, and where clients demand the best of them every day. In every organization I've led, people are the only true assets. In real terms, that means business performance is directly correlated with the performance of the team and the individuals in it. Sure, that holds true for just about every business, but in professional services like consulting, it's hard-coded. The rates you charge, the work you win, the extent to which clients are willing to place their trust in you and your team, and the quality of support you provide are completely dependent on the capabilities and strengths of your people.

Where does feedback enter this picture? Well, without meaningful feedback and coaching, my people don't grow, and they don't succeed. And if my people don't succeed, neither does my business. Given the fact that I have a long track record of developing great consultants and thriving organizations, I must be the Queen of Feedback, right?

Wrong. I'm the first to admit that I also have work to do. What's more, my own organization sometimes struggles to meet its aspirational goal of sustaining a culture of open and candid feedback.

Trying to understand the dichotomy between my feedback shortcomings and my success in developing people and organizations has led me to explore my experiences with and beliefs about feedback. The conclusions I've come to are reflected not only in the ideas I'll share with you, but also in the habits and practices that my people and I apply every day in our work.

Here are a few of the bedrock ideas that feature prominently throughout this book:

MANY OF OUR BELIEFS AND IDEAS ABOUT FEEDBACK ARE INCORRECT AND COUNTERPRODUCTIVE AND HAVE LONG BEEN DISTORTED BY OUR EXPERIENCES.

- » It's time we clear up some age-old misconceptions about feedback that continue to influence us today. In fact, it's time to embrace a new working definition of feedback.
- » A basic understanding of the science behind our reactions to feedback will help us move forward in a new, more effective way.

AS I PROPOSE IN THE TITLE, THERE IS A WAY TO FIX FEEDBACK AND PUT OUR FEAR OF IT BEHIND US.

- » Doing this will require a movement in which we all work together to fix feedback.
- » Simple ideas, conversation models, and tips and tricks can help us build our feedback muscle, both individually and collectively.

TO DEVELOP INDIVIDUALS AND BUILD TEAMS THAT THRIVE, GROW, AND OPERATE AT OPTIMUM LEVELS OF PERFORMANCE, WE MUST START WITH TRUST.

- » Trust is built over time through human connections that are kind and supportive, and that sends a strong message that *we're in this together.*
- » Trust isn't built in a day; it's an ongoing process that influences how we show up in every conversation, decision, and action.

I hope this book will inspire you to join our movement to redefine and reboot feedback, because together we have the power to shape the world of work into a more connected and more inspiring place. How much more will we achieve as individuals and organizations if we can make that a reality? How much happier will we all be when feedback is no longer a dirty word?

F##DB@CK!

CHAPTER 1

FEEDBACK HAS
A BRANDING PROBLEM

IF OUR MARKETING COLLEAGUES were to do a branding assessment on feedback it would not score well. This should surprise no one, since it's been mishandled for centuries by most of humanity. We've built its horrible brand one lousy experience at a time. You know what I mean: using feedback to punish, shame, or manipulate. Saving it up and then heaping a big load of it on an unsuspecting employee. Letting our biases influence our perspectives. Insisting on sharing, even if it's clearly the wrong place and time. Telling one colleague, who tells another colleague, who finally tells the person we were beefing about what we said. Thinking that brutal frankness is the best approach or that passive-aggressive insinuation will get our point across. Sharing only when we want to make it clear that something, or someone, didn't meet our expectations.

And it's not just those offering feedback who are to blame. Think about how often we lash out defensively when we're presented with feedback. We argue the facts, we change the subject to the messenger's faults, or we get mad and stomp off in a huff. Maybe we listen quietly, then simply shut down. Or, worse yet, we don't listen at all.

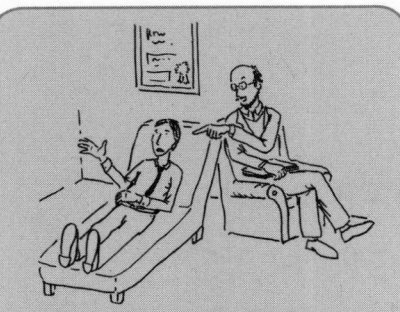

As you were reading the examples of situations that have given feedback its bad brand, did it occur to you how many of them crop up in the dreaded annual performance review? Too many, too often. In my first book, I share the eight flaws of traditional performance management. Fatal Flaw #2 notes that nobody opens up to the person who pokes them in the eye (and when poor feedback techniques are deployed, it's no wonder). Even more disconcerting is the fact that those negative annual review experiences often taint the relationship between the employee and their manager for the balance of the year, and maybe for the entirety of their working relationship. Bad feedback memories have a long, long half-life. More on that later.

And how often do we actually seek out feedback when we're stewing on questions like "Am I on the right track in my handling of this project?" or "Could I have done a better job of facilitating that meeting this morning?" For most of us, the instinct is to sit back and wait for someone to give us feedback instead of asking for it.

The root of feedback's branding problem lies in the way we're thinking about it and experiencing it. It's time to examine the habits we've formed, the approaches we've adopted, and the stories we tell ourselves. If so many of us are walking around wounded by our feedback experiences, then it's obvious that we're doing it wrong as a culture. We've got our work cut out for us: rebranding feedback as something we want to run toward and not away from is going to require some serious changes to both our heads and our hearts.

HOW FEEDBACK LOST ITS WAY

Bad Habits Learned Early

We learn habits early, both good and bad, from those around us. And, despite our best intentions, we tend to perpetuate learned behaviors or techniques, including those that may have irked us when we were on the receiving end of them.

These early lessons influence our perception of feedback, since we've grown up observing, receiving, and shelling it out in ways that too often hurt much more than they help. At its worst, it comes at us in the form of criticisms, angry words, and personal judgments. This harsh form of feedback (or, more accurately, what we've gotten used to calling feedback) is often what we experience when we're young, be it from our parents, our siblings, kids on the playground, or those early (and often horrible) bosses. As a result, we're conditioned from the get-go to see feedback as a negative force and a source of fear, and since most of us perceive feedback as a negative concept, we're much less likely to offer it or seek it out. This aversion becomes so strong that, even when feedback is good (meaning it's positive reinforcement or redirection that's easy to take in), we may not even recognize it as feedback.

Our bosses, parents, teachers, friends, and siblings probably didn't set out to do us harm (well, maybe some of our siblings did). They were just influenced by models of feedback that are rooted in our general societal misconceptions. My point is this: we each have a legacy of feedback that is imprinted on us at an early age, and it's rarely a pretty picture. Letting go of the fear means unlearning the habits that got us here and abandoning the misguided ideas and approaches that have been ingrained in us over the years.

Nothing, Nothing, and Then . . . Boom!

As I've made clear, I'm no fan of the traditional performance review. Not only have traditional annual reviews failed to deliver better performance, they've also done much to taint our perception of what real feedback is. They've trained us to believe that feedback is a big event, something ominous, confrontational, and laden with hidden intentions.

The ritual of the annual review tells us (erroneously) that feedback is what you get when you sit down with your manager behind a closed door, talk about the things that have gone well (we hope), and then discuss your areas for improvement and perhaps how much money you'll be getting the following year. The mission of the manager is often to tally up and dutifully document your wins and losses for the year and provide you with an assessment of your worth, often in comparison with your peers. It's likely to be much more of a monologue than a dialogue, and it's easily biased by influences like recency (the tendency to perceive more recent events as being more impactful than those that are further in the past), and the idiosyncratic rater effect of the manager.[1] It requires the participants to mentally "suit up" for battle, and it smacks of positional power, so it rarely feels relaxed or collaborative. When it's over you quickly forget all the positive takeaways, and instead you obsess about your reviewer's assessments of your areas for improvement, contemplating whether they were relevant, fair, or even truly representative of your work. This construct, pounded into us by years of annual reviews, has had a toxic influence on our relationship with feedback.

It's time to reimagine feedback as a fluid and ongoing conversation, free of ratings, angst, and judgment. As we move forward, it will also be crucial to recognize the fact that we're all getting more feedback than we realize, but that it may not register as feedback when it comes without the sting. Any time a single insight is shared in the moment—even when the manager's door is open and no one is worried about following an agenda or creating a paper trail—that is feedback. And it's probably far more digestible and effective than the overwhelming information dump you received during your annual review.

The Feedback Paradox

Surprisingly, the most common complaint we hear about feedback is, "I don't get enough." This tells us that despite feedback's damaged brand most of us still crave it and intuitively know that it's a good thing—when it's done right. However, even when we take into account all the "unregistered" feedback we've been receiving, most of us are still experiencing a feedback deficit. A 2018 Office Vibe "Global State of Employee Engagement" study[2] found that 62 percent of employees want more feedback from their colleagues, and 83 percent said they appreciate feedback, be it positive or negative. This is the paradox: despite the mess we've made of it, most of us want more feedback, yet few of us make a habit of actively seeking or extending it. Feedback begets feedback, but somebody needs to help get this ball rolling. What if that somebody were you?

MOVEMENT

CHAPTER 2

OUR MOVEMENT TO FIX FEEDBACK

DECLARATION #1: Feedback should *be a good thing*. When we take a step back and think about its true intent, we realize that feedback shouldn't be a bad thing. If we as humans want to improve, grow, and advance, we need insights that can help us move in the right direction. If we close ourselves off from understanding how others experience us, then we close ourselves off to a life of learning and growth.

DECLARATION #2: To make feedback a good thing, change is needed. In the first chapter, we shared with you the reason why not enough of us experience feedback as a positive force. In short, we're feeling the pain we've been inflicting on one another and ourselves over the centuries. If we're going to break this cycle, we need to change the what, how, and when of engaging in the process. In other words, we need to create our own movement to fix feedback.

MAKING THE CASE FOR CHANGE

I'm ready, I'm ready, I'm ready!
—SPONGEBOB SQUAREPANTS

You've heard it a million times, but that's only because it's true: the first step in any change is acknowledging the need for change. But the sad fact is that we're all a bit reluctant to get out of our ruts, so we're usually slow to move until something stirs our emotions enough to make it seem worth tackling.

How about you? Are you ready to change? As you read the examples of feedback gone awry in chapter 1, did you wince as some hit a little too close to home? Did you start compiling a mental list of the times you failed to ask for insights, shut someone down who was genuinely trying to help, complained to your lunch buddies about working with a certain peer, slid a recommendation for improvement between a few half-hearted compliments, or jumped to assumptions before seeking to understand?

Don't beat yourself up. Remember that I'm right there with you. I can't tell you how many times in researching and writing this book I've found myself cringing as I reflect on things I've done, said, not said, not asked, or imposed upon others. While it's easy to point fingers at all those who have made you grind your teeth and clench your fists, it takes far more courage to stand up and admit to your own mistakes. We need to acknowledge them, learn from them, and then press on, knowing better.

If we're going to change feedback in a fundamental way, then we need to make this a movement, a seismic philosophical shift in our thinking about feedback, rather than a simple tune-up of our delivery methods. We all need to become seekers of information and truth that will help us contribute to the team, the project, the cause we're a part of. Managers and leaders, that starts with you. We'll be asking you to step away from the traditional feedback roles of "knower" and "teller" and slide comfortably into the roles of explorer and learner. This movement will prod us out of what we now know to be the danger zone of telling others what they need to do to change, and into a zone of collaboration where we figure it out together.

By reading this book you're taking the first step toward becoming a leader in this movement. I'm calling on you to convince others of the need for change, inform them of our purpose (creating a world where feedback helps, not hurts), and model behaviors that make it easier for them to join in. We'll need to appeal to both the hearts and the minds of those we're asking to join us. The following sections provide four compelling arguments we hope will do just that.

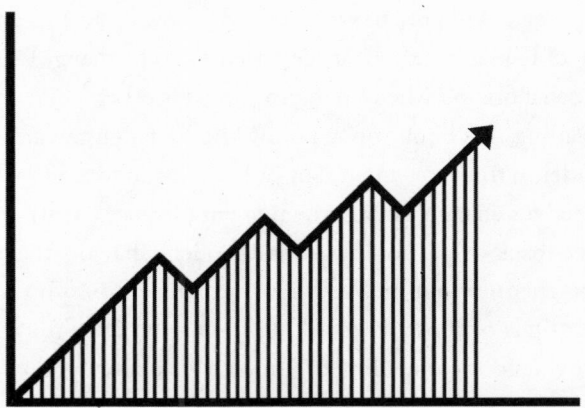

MEANINGFUL AND MEASURABLE OUTCOMES FOR YOUR BUSINESS

The numbers back up our call for change. New research shows that improving our approach to feedback drives meaningfully improved performance for both businesses and individuals. Let's begin with a quick dive into the data at the organizational level. In 2018, the Institute for Corporate Performance (i4cp) and the Center for Effective Organizations (CEO) published a joint study called "Performance Feedback Culture Drives Business Impact."[1] In it they looked at the impact of various techniques that are often used to improve performance management effectiveness. They found that the top driver of measurable improvement was the adoption of a Performance Feedback Culture (PFC). Their study notes that "PFC is established and nurtured by company practices that focus managers' attention on doing performance feedback effectively: regular and varied communication, training on how to do it well, modeling by senior executives in how they do it for their subordinates, rewards and recognition for doing it well, monitoring getting it done, and manager selection and promotion based on excellent performance feedback competencies." When these elements are in place the results are compelling.

The study looked at 57 publicly traded U.S. companies and compared the results for the top third based on the PFC measurement factors with those of the bottom third. The top third had financial results that were double those of the bottom third, including net profit margin, return on investment, return on assets, and return on equity. Additional learnings from the study reinforce the impact of developmental and ongoing feedback, noting that these two factors had the highest relationship to influencing, developing, motivating, and retaining employees. Another branch of this research looked at organizations that are privately held, foreign, not-for-profit, and/or government organizations. They correlated Glassdoor's Employer Brand Score for these organizations with the same survey variables. Interestingly, "only one of the predictor variables was significant." Which one? You guessed it: organizational emphasis on developmental, rather than evaluative, feedback.

In the end, the study concludes what we've been advocating in our PM Reboot work for years and the idea that was at the center of my previous book: "Performance management is ineffective for companies that have a weak performance feedback culture. . . . Performance management that is focused on employee-oriented outcomes (including employee development, employee motivation, and employee retention), not performance management that is focused on organizational outcomes, leads to financial success."

MEANINGFUL AND MEASURABLE OUTCOMES FOR YOUR PEOPLE

Now let's pivot to examine the data at the human level. I'm intrigued by a series of studies[2] conducted by Gretchen Spreitzer and Christine Porath, in collaboration with the Ross School of Business's Center for Positive Organizations. They interviewed more than 1,200 employees, measuring key metrics related to performance and behavior. Their studies included white-collar and blue-collar workers across multiple industries. They concluded that thriving employees, "those not just satisfied and productive but also engaged in creating the future—the companies' and their own," demonstrated better performance than their peers. White-collar workers scored 16 percent higher and blue-collar workers scored 27 percent higher in overall performance. Thriving employees also demonstrated notably better health and 125 percent less burnout. What's more, they were 32 percent more committed to their organizations and 46 percent more satisfied with their jobs.

The research found two factors that drive an individual's ability to thrive: vitality and learning. Vitality is defined as "the sense of being alive, passionate, and excited," while learning is "the growth that comes from gaining new knowledge and skills." At its simplest level, vitality comes from a strong sense that what we do makes a difference, while learning means we're building our skills and capabilities while simultaneously boosting our confidence in our potential growth.

I don't think it's hard to understand the connection between vitality and learning and feedback. Significant drivers of vitality include relationships, connections, recognition, and clarity—all outcomes of healthy, ongoing feedback conversations. Learning is the result of insights we gain that help us improve, expand, and advance. These are also outcomes of trusted and specific feedback relevant to our growth. So, if we're looking to drive stronger performance from—and better experiences for—our people, it seems we would want to fuel their sense of vitality and learning. What better way to do that than with inspiring and insightful feedback?

UPPING YOUR LEADERSHIP IMPACT
FOR YOU AND YOUR TEAM

Simple fact: leadership is vital to performance. Effective leaders improve performance, while poor leaders drive disengagement and weaker performance. There are shelves of research-based books on leadership, so we don't need to dwell on the subject here. What's relevant to our movement is understanding feedback's influence on the quality and impact of leadership and employee engagement.

If you've been looking for the secret sauce to increase your effectiveness as a leader, you can stop looking: it's feedback!

> How you as a leader ask for and extend feedback has a direct correlation with your impact on and respect among those you lead.

Jack Zenger and Joe Folkman have conducted several highly recognized studies related to leadership and feedback. They've had so much influence on my thinking that you'll see their findings sprinkled throughout this book. One study[3] that included 22,719 leaders looked at the relationship between feedback and employee engagement. The link between a leader's ability to give honest feedback and employee engagement is stunning. Zenger and Folkman found that those leaders who ranked in the bottom 10 percent for giving honest feedback had teams that ranked 25 percent lower in engagement than their peers. Conversely, leaders in the top 10 percent for giving honest feedback had teams in the top quartile for engagement.

A corollary to this finding, also noted by Zenger and Folkman, is that leaders often hold incorrect and impact-limiting beliefs about feedback. Unfortunately, too many leaders mistake the concept of honest and direct feedback with telling people and teams only what's going wrong. (I believe there's some old-school, 1950s thinking fueling this idea that good managers and leaders are tough and never satisfied.) Leaders who fall victim to these false ideas tend to either avoid feedback altogether so as not to appear to be the bad guy or gal, or they gain a reputation as a criticizer due to their propensity for quickly pointing out flaws. Interestingly, the research concludes that effective leaders are those who demonstrate a preference for positive feedback. Positive feedback is not only the best tool for developing your people, but it also reflects well on you as a leader.

Another Zenger and Folkman study[4] looked at the relationship between asking for feedback and overall leadership effectiveness. This time they studied more than 50,000 leaders and found that those who were ranked in the top 10 percent for asking for feedback were in the 86th percentile for overall leadership effectiveness. Sadly, those wallowing in the bottom 10 percent for asking were also wallowing in the bottom ranks for effectiveness at the 15th percentile.

I've just thrown a lot of information at you about the connection between leadership and feedback. What should you conclude from all that data? If you're a leader looking to increase your impact, influence, team engagement, and thereby the performance of your team, then get your "ask" on, make the practice of sharing feedback a priority, and put a strong emphasis on positive feedback. Any executive or HR leader who's looking to influence organizational performance should help their leaders make a habit of asking for and giving feedback, and frequently recognizing the great work of their teams and people.

Why do we see such a strong connection between feedback and the performance of leaders and teams? Here are a few compelling reasons to consider:

INSIGHTS = GROWTH. If feedback provides the knowledge necessary to improve and grow, then you as a leader need it just as much as anyone else. This is where courage and humility come into the picture. You may have to set your ego and self-doubt aside and admit that having been chosen for a leadership role doesn't mean you're done growing and learning. In fact, it might mean you have a whole lot more to learn, given your expanded responsibilities and influence.

> » Feedback is also the knowledge that helps your people grow and thrive. Creating a culture in which you and your team are better at sharing helpful feedback is key to driving performance and engagement at both the individual and team levels. It can unlock innovation and increase shared learning, both very good things. Your job as the leader is to go first. You'll need to carry the flag for your own feedback movement.

KNOW WHAT NEEDS FIXING. Your job as a leader is to make it easy for your team to get work done. But how can you do that if you don't know what's getting in the way? And how do you find out? It's simple: you ask.

TRUSTED RELATIONSHIPS THROUGH CONVERSATION. Later, we'll dig into the importance of relationships and connections as foundations for both positive and improvement-oriented feedback conversations. When I see my clients or employees struggle, I remind them that talking, listening, asking—the daily conversations that build relationships and trust—act as the connective tissue that holds an organization together and makes it strong. And it's this trust, built on ongoing communication, that's reflected in those leadership effectiveness scores.

MAKING MEANINGFUL CONNECTIONS

Has anyone ever pulled you aside, scheduled a special lunch, or sent you a handwritten note to express their appreciation for something you told them that made a difference in their life? Looking back on three decades of interaction with clients, peers, and employees, those moments are the most meaningful and a big part of what makes this challenging career I've selected so gratifying.

The stories are all unique in their own way. Some might tell me I brought clarity at a time when they needed it, or perhaps I shone a spotlight on a challenge that led them in a new or better career direction. And sometimes it's been about little things: a casual suggestion, a reflection on something they did well, or a simple word to them to soldier on and be encouraged by the impact they're making.

I treasure those moments. Who wouldn't? But I also treasure the times when someone cared enough to take a risk and tell me something I needed to hear. In my early days of leading Arthur Andersen's Pacific Northwest consulting practice, one of my senior managers took a moment during our weekly drive down to a client to tell me, kindly but firmly, to quit holding back, take the bull by the horns, and get on with leading the practice. I've always reflected on that conversation as a turning point in my own trajectory. Similarly, after several years at Hitachi Consulting when I was struggling to stay engaged, one of my close colleagues who was supporting a special project I was working on noted she hadn't seen me so excited in years. She casually mentioned that, when I was talking about a new people-centered service line I wanted Hitachi to launch, my enthusiasm was contagious. It turns out that her comment, combined with a few other events, opened my eyes to the idea of building my own practice, one focused on people. That service line was never adopted by Hitachi, but it did bloom a few years later as PeopleFirm.

What's most striking in each of these cases is the influence that our words can have on one another. They have the power to inspire, to unlock potential, to lift us up instead of knocking us down. If that doesn't get you onboard with this movement, then nothing will.

FEAR

CHAPTER 3

WHAT SCIENCE TELLS US

WE'RE ALL FAMILIAR WITH President Franklin Delano Roosevelt's Depression-era assurance that "the only thing we have to fear is fear itself." Roosevelt understood how fear can paralyze, demoralize, and divide individuals and groups who need to pull together in the face of a collective threat.

When it comes to feedback, it's not a collective threat we're facing; it's a collective opportunity to open new doors that lead to bigger and better outcomes. However, fear has long limited the important role that feedback should be playing in our working lives. And that fear is the result of feedback gone wrong. It's paralyzed the flow of good, helpful communication; it's demoralized well-intentioned people and, by extension, entire organizations; and it's too often produced divisions instead of healing them. Why do we fear it, and how do we fix it? The answers to both these questions lie in understanding the evolutionary legacy that dictates our biological responses to intense physical or emotional situations. Armed with an awareness of the complex set of defense mechanisms we employ to avoid or escape those encounters, we can then retrain our minds and rethink our ways of interacting to take the fear out of feedback once and for all.

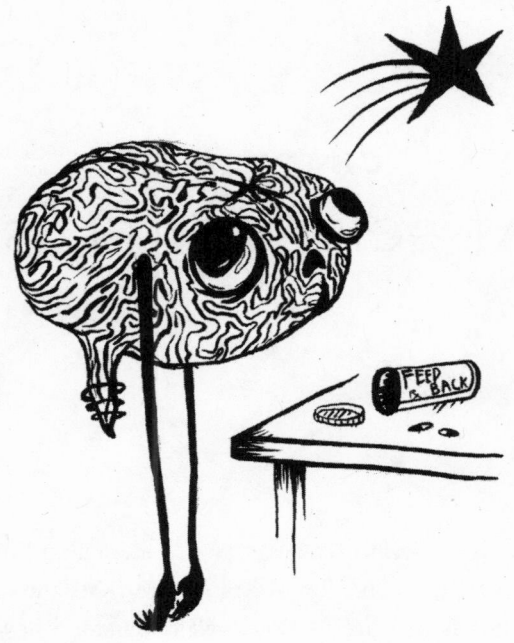

YOUR BRAIN ON FEEDBACK

Meet Steven, a smart, thoughtful, and talented fellow, and Mira, his equally capable and caring manager. One morning, Mira says, "I've got some feedback for you, Steven. Would you step into my office?"

Hearing this sets Steven's heart racing. His palms begin to sweat as his numb legs carry him toward Mira's office. A series of questions, all negative, flash through his brain: *Why me? What the heck is this about, anyway? Did I mess up or forget something? Is she out to get me? Is everyone in the office out to get me? Am I getting fired???*

Steven and Mira have always had a cordial (if superficial) working relationship, and he has no logical reason to suspect her of ill will. So why is his reaction so extreme, so immediate, and so overwhelmingly negative? The answer can be found in the past—not only Steven's, but all humankind's as well.

Not everyone will react to a simple offering of feedback as dramatically as Steven has, but the fact is that most of us will experience some variation of his distress. Like too many of us, Steven's brain has been conditioned to go into "fight, flight, or freeze" mode at the mere mention of the word "feedback." Some of Steven's previous experiences with feedback have been rough, so this moment sets off a powerful and rapid fear response in his amygdala (what we'll call the "primitive brain"), which triggers his sympathetic nervous system to activate a powerful cocktail of stress hormones and neurotransmitters that prompt his body to go into hyperdrive.

This "fight, flight, or freeze" response is an evolutionary adaptation that was essential to the survival of the human species when massive predators and other existential threats were abundant. Your face flushes and your mouth dries out as blood flow is diverted from surface tissues to your arms and legs, and your muscles tense and tremble in anticipation of confronting or escaping the source of the threat. Your heartbeat and breathing accelerate, pumping oxygen-rich blood through your system to fuel quick action. Your hearing sharpens, and your pupils dilate as a kind of tunnel vision kicks in, creating a hyperaware, highly reactive state.

It's an extreme response shaped by eons of extreme circumstances. The problem is that our brains have evolved much more slowly than our society has. Sure, this acute stress response still serves its purpose if you're escaping a burning building or taking fast action to avoid a car accident. But it can also be triggered when the threat is emotional and not physical, since the brain doesn't always register them as different types of threats. And when our primitive brains respond to emotional triggers by prioritizing physical strength and narrowing our focus on survival over reason and emotional control, we're liable to lash out, run for proverbial cover, shut down, or resort to appeasement (become a "pleaser") in order to relieve the emotional discomfort that's built up inside us. In any case, there's a disconnect between who we'd like to be in that moment and who we show up as.

While "fight, flight, or freeze" is the well-known shorthand for the acute stress response, there's actually a fourth choice that's become common both in and out of the workplace: the appease response. It's a means of deflecting when the situation overwhelms your capacity to cope. We Seattleites would recognize this passive-aggressive defense mechanism as a variation on "Northwest nice." No matter where you live, you've surely witnessed the weak smile and the half-hearted agreement that masks the implicit message, "Sure, whatever you say. Can I go now?" When this emotional emergency parachute is deployed in a feedback situation, it can appear that the message has been received when it's really fallen on deaf ears.

Not surprisingly, this disconnect spells disaster for Steven and Mira. Here's what results:

ZERO TRUST. Since Steven feels threatened, his "fight, flight, or freeze" response kicks into high gear, so he's not inclined to trust Mira. This creates a powerful, negative emotional imprint of this response. His brain stores this encounter for future reference, meaning the results of his next feedback experience might be even worse.

ZERO TRUTH. Stuck in this state, Steven will fail to see, appreciate, or process any legitimate feedback Mira tries to convey.

ZERO PERSPECTIVE. Steven may catastrophize. The human brain tends to make one thing into everything, especially when it comes to negative input. A suggestion on improving performance becomes *Uh-oh, my career's in trouble.* A rejected idea is quickly translated into *They don't value me here.*

Is there anything we can do to bring our calmest, most collaborative selves to the feedback table? As a matter of fact, there is, though the answer may seem counterintuitive. In order to free our minds to fully engage, we must calm the stress response. We will never be entirely free of it, but we can manage it in order to optimize our responses to feedback and the opportunities it presents. Look at it as getting out of our brains and into our bodies for a while. That means developing a keener awareness of our physical responses in the moment and learning how to influence them.

Each time we participate in a challenging conversation with greater calm and heightened self-awareness, we create or reinforce neural pathways in our brains that will allow for more positive responses under stress in the future. The better we get at handling our fear (in this case, the fear of feedback), the less threatening these situations become.

When you feel yourself getting caught in an emotional vortex, the goal is to shift as much of your attention as you can to your body and your senses for at least 10 seconds or for three full breaths. Easing fear, anxiety, and anger (common emotions when the primitive brain is fired up) by becoming consciously aware of your physical sensations requires that your prefrontal cortex (also known as the "wise brain") be engaged. Science tells us that you can't be "located" in both of these parts of the brain at once. In other words, you can't simply think yourself out of the stress response. You must shift your awareness to your physical body in order to ease the stress response and allow your wise brain to regain control. Training our brains to build these new pathways and ingraining new, healthier habits doesn't happen at the snap of a finger, so stay patient and positive as you explore the following suggestions for mitigating the "fight, flight, or freeze" response:

FEEL YOUR FEET. Flatten them hard into the floor. Feel your toes touching the ground. How do your feet feel? Soft? Numb? Warm? Tingly? Keep feeling the physical sensation as you slowly breathe in and out a few times.

LISTEN TO THE SOUNDS AROUND YOU. Shift your focus to the sounds around you. Can you hear the click of computer keys, or the murmur of traffic or chirping of birds outside? Listen. Focus your attention on these sounds and try to keep it there for 10 seconds.

RINSE AND REPEAT. You can groove new neural pathways by turning to these exercises anytime you feel stressed. With practice it should get easier and easier to shift your focus and clear your mind.

Shirzad Chamine, Stanford University professor and author of *Positive Intelligence,* calls practices like these "Positivity Quotient reps" and suggests we practice them for 10 seconds, 100 times a day. (Sound too daunting? That's only about 15 minutes.)[1]

DON'T FORGET TO BREATHE

Here's a slightly more complex exercise that may help you tamp down the agitating effects of the stress response. 4-7-8 breathing is a simple relaxation practice developed by Dr. Andrew Weil. Working from the lungs outward, techniques like 4-7-8 can rebalance the flow of oxygen in your body. This can come to your aid in a stressful feedback moment, and also provide daily relief from the accumulated stress and anxiety that can keep you from being at your best when taking in or giving feedback.

1. Rest the tip of your tongue against the roof of your mouth, right behind your teeth. Allow your lips to part.
2. Exhale completely through your mouth.
3. Next, close your lips, inhaling silently through your nose as you count to 4 in your head.
4. Then, for 7 seconds, hold your breath. (This may seem like a long time at first!) Holding your breath slows your heart rate and causes your body to relax and your mind to slow down.
5. Exhale through your mouth (go ahead, make it loud) for 8 seconds.
6. When you inhale again, you start another round.

Of course, the long-term solution for taking the stress response out of the feedback equation lies in the success of our movement to create a world where feedback is no longer a source of such anxiety. That's not going to be easy, since fear finds so many opportunities to sink its claws into every member of the feedback ecosystem.

WHAT WE REALLY FEAR

Feedback is far from a life-or-death proposition. So why does it trigger such extreme reactions? What is the big F'ing deal about feedback, anyway? What exactly is the threat that lurks in the feedback shadows, firing up our primitive brains like a crouched saber-toothed tiger ready to pounce?

When we peel back the layers and look closely at what frightens us about feedback, it boils down to this: identity and connection. Yes, at the heart of our fear is our identity, and how that identity is shaped and reinforced by our connections to and affiliations with the rest of the world. What we truly fear are isolation, ostracism, and abandonment. And while isolation meant almost certain death for our ancestors, today the physical implications are considerably far less dire. Yet, for most of us, the desire to belong is a prime motivator. Humans are social beings; we instinctively want to be included and valued. The need to stay connected with and accepted by our communities drives our actions without our intellectual complicity.

So, what do we do? We seek protection.

> The only way to avoid mistakes and criticism: say nothing, do nothing, be nothing.
> —Adapted from a quote by Elbert Hubbard, *Olympians: Elbert Hubbard's Selected Writings, Part 2*

We protect ourselves through avoidance, and we protect ourselves through distortion. We take false comfort in believing that what we don't hear or don't say can't hurt us. We avoid seeking insights that we might not want to hear. We avoid sharing perspectives that might damage connections with those we hold in esteem (like our boss, for example, not the guy who just cut us off on the freeway). We avoid fully assimilating what's been shared so we can manage the risk that it might challenge our ideas of who we are and how we're perceived by the crowd or those whom we value. And often we distort what we hear to better fit our own frameworks and views, again with the aim of preserving our self-image and our connections. These behaviors or reactions are especially true when we're unprepared for the critical feedback that comes our way.

Interestingly, this self-protective behavior prevents us from extending feedback at least as much as it prevents us from seeking it. Most of us don't want to hurt those we care about, so we tend to delay or even completely avoid sharing a thought or an idea that we suspect might upset the recipient and potentially damage our relationship.

Let's revisit our friends Steven and Mira, but this time, let's consider Mira's dilemma. What Steven doesn't realize is that Mira has avoided this conversation for as long as she could. A recent project postmortem called out the shortcomings of Steven's work on the project. The postmortem participants asked Mira to make sure Steven received the feedback. Intellectually, Mira knows that if she gives him this coaching it will help him be more impactful to the new project he's working on. At the same time, she wants to maintain her status as a smart, savvy, and likable manager in the eyes of both her peers and Steven. So, though she's the one who initiated this interaction and would appear to be in the driver's seat, she's confronting her own proverbial sabertooth. As the meeting draws closer and closer, the negative chatter in her head escalates: *Am I sure that what I'm going to tell him is true and fair? What exactly did they want me to say again, anyway? I'm afraid this is not going to go well. What if he gets angry? What if he quits? Maybe I'm not that good at managing people after all.*

Fear and anxiety are clouding Mira's judgment, so by the time she sits down with Steven, she's made a set of assumptions that will make her ill-equipped to have a conversation that welcomes give-and-take and exploration. She's considering one of two paths at this point:

- On Path One, she's ready to "yell, tell, or sell" her way through the conversation and get out quickly. She'll exit feeling a little adrenaline rush for getting that off her list and meeting her commitment to her peers. Steven, on the other hand, will leave smarting.
- On Path Two, she gives Steven some love, timidly slides in the feedback she wanted to share, then returns to more positive topics before wrapping up the conversation. She'll leave hoping he got the message and relieved that she avoided any conflict. Steven will walk away perplexed over exactly what she was trying to get across and why.

Both paths lead to a lose-lose outcome. Steven and Mira each enter this interaction in fear's grip, and fear wins out, creating a poor experience for both that will ultimately diminish any trust that may have existed between them. Because both are focused on avoidance, the main thing they end up avoiding is a healthy, productive dialogue. What occurs instead is a fiasco that reinforces their tainted notions of what feedback is.

As mentioned in the foreword, digging into this topic has been a challenge even for me. In other words, I can be as clunky as anyone when it comes to feedback. I've come to realize that my high degree of empathy (yes, I'm known to cry during especially touching dog food commercials and while watching strangers bid a tearful goodbye in the airport) was seriously influencing my own engagement with feedback. In short, it was driving my reluctance to share tougher feedback with others, even when that feedback would truly help them. I was confusing my relationships, and the care I had for them, with the intent of the feedback. Letting go of that reluctance has improved my capability to extend feedback. Honestly, it will always be something I'll need to work on, but I keep reminding myself that the best thing I can do for the people I truly care about is to help them grow and improve. That entails both upping my quota of encouragement and support for those around me (something I like doing anyway) and identifying the right moments to redirect or challenge when needed to help them go further.

WHY DO WE GO
POSITIVELY NEGATIVE?

There's plenty of science that explains why both Steven and Mira seem so resigned to listening to the worst version of their inner voice.

Here's what we know:

- Our brains process negative information faster than other stimuli.
- Negative information has more influence in evaluations than positive information.
- We weigh negative impacts or outcomes more heavily than equivalent positive outcomes (e.g., we react more dramatically to losing 20 dollars than we do to finding 20 dollars).
- We're more motivated to avoid bad definitions of ourselves than to seek good ones.
- Negative information gets far more processing time than good information.
- We form negative opinions more rapidly and are slower to let them go.
- We remember negative events far longer than we remember positive ones.
- In nearly every situation, research tells us that bad is stronger than good.[2]

> For good to prevail over bad, it must win by the numbers. One bad against many good.

It all boils down to this: events we perceive as bad produce more emotion, have bigger impacts, and longer-lasting effects. Why? It's human nature, that's why. Again, our instincts for self-protection play a big role. Our ancestors' survival was dependent on their awareness of and speed at responding to negative signals, triggering them to take defensive action and seek self-preservation. Research also links our negativity bias to factors beyond our evolution, like the ways in which humans process and react to trauma, how we learn, and our impulse to adhere to social pressures. For our purposes, we don't need to debate the causes. What's important is to build our awareness of this phenomenon and understand how this knowledge can help us fix feedback.

THE VELCRO/TEFLON PHENOMENON

Our tendency to remember the bad and forget or dismiss the good is often described as the Velcro/Teflon phenomenon. When you receive negative stimuli, it sticks in your brain as if it were made of Velcro. On the other hand, when positive information arrives, it's likely to slide off as easily as a fried egg in a Teflon pan.

Each of us can easily and quickly recall feedback that left us licking our wounds. This is often our negative bias at work. Overall, it's likely that we've been on the receiving end of an equal if not greater amount of positive feedback, but those experiences are harder to recall. Just recognizing this natural human tendency is powerful in itself. It helps us understand why we're great at inflicting pain on ourselves when we overweigh, overprocess, and generally spin on input we perceive as negative. This recognition can also help us tune into our own negative biases when considering how to deliver feedback to others, or whether or not we should risk the possible pain of seeking it out.

Here's an example of negativity bias at work: Let's say you received a 5 out of 5 on your performance review in June. (Again, I'm no fan of ratings or performance reviews, but they're useful components of this example.) That 5 is supposed to be cause for celebration, isn't it? Then why is it you left that review feeling let down? Was it the suggestion made by your manager that you could have handled that situation back in February a little better? Has your mind been churning on that comment ever since? Have you spent too many lunches complaining to your coworkers about how your manager completely missed the context of February's situation? Did the praise you heard get forgotten? In fleeting moments of clarity, you might remember that you did receive the highest rating, that your pay increase was at the top of the band, and that your new assignment reflects the confidence your manager has in your abilities. But that negative feedback still rankles. If you've ever walked away from a review or any other generally positive experience with a piece of negative feedback stuck in your craw, then you need to tune in and consider that negativity bias may be impairing your ability to take in the good and accurately assess what's been offered.

IT'S ONLY TEMPORARY

Are you an optimist or a pessimist? Do you realize it's a choice? Interestingly, this choice plays an important role in how we engage with perceived negative input. When we hold on to the negative for too long, or even worse, forever, it limits our potential and strips us of the inner strength to move forward. In his book *Learned Optimism: How to Change Your Mind and Your Life*, Martin Seligman (the father of positive psychology) warns us against making negative events "permanent, personal, or pervasive." People who are more pessimistic are likely to hear feedback in a way that feels permanent (*I've always been this way*), pervasive (*I suck at everything*), and personal (*Why am I the guy who always gets the negative feedback?*). If we can change our listening and our thinking to be more optimistic, then we can improve our ability to hear the feedback as "temporary" (*Well, I'll do better next time*), situational (*That was a pretty tough environment to succeed in*), and specific (*Okay, this one attempt did not go well*).

It's within your power to choose.

> When making your choice you may want to consider this anecdote from Seth Godin: Poet Donald Hall told the story of a hermit in New Hampshire, a man who passed away leaving behind sheds full of hoarded stuff. In one of the sheds was a box labeled, "string too short to be saved." That's what we do with the trivia that gets in the way of our best work. The tiny slights, the small rejections, the bumps in the road that could be easily forgotten. Ideas too useless to be saved. But we save them nonetheless. This is the cruft that keeps us from moving forward. What happens when we treasure the memories that serve as fuel, and ignore the rest?

MINDSET MATTERS

The seminal work of Dr. Carol Dweck, a Stanford psychologist, concluded that mindset matters when it comes to performance and learning. Her work, synthesized in *Mindset: The New Psychology of Success*,[3] is an inquiry into the power of our beliefs, both conscious and unconscious, and how changing even the simplest of them can have a profound impact on nearly every aspect of our lives. A mindset, according to Dweck, is a self-perception or "self-theory" that people hold about themselves. When describing how humans approach life, challenges, and performance, Dweck coined the terms "fixed mindset" and "growth mindset."

> "I don't divide the world into the weak and the strong, or the successes and failures. . . . I divide the world into learners and nonlearners."
> —Benjamin Barber, eminent sociologist

According to Dweck, "In a fixed mindset, people believe their basic qualities, like their intelligence or talent, are simply fixed traits. They spend their time documenting their intelligence or talent instead of developing them. They also believe that talent alone creates success—without effort." Alternatively, "In a growth mindset, people believe that their most basic abilities can be developed through dedication and hard work—brains and talent are just the starting point. This view creates a love of learning and a resilience that is essential for great accomplishment." To bottom-line it, mindset is a key factor in influencing our potential to grow and improve.

Research has shown that individuals with a growth mindset (those who believe their talents can be developed) tend to achieve more than those with a more fixed mindset (those who believe their talents are innate gifts). Dweck's research[4] found that several factors influence this higher achievement outcome. Some of the notable behaviors are summarized in the table below:

FIXED MINDSET VS. GROWTH MINDSET

	Fixed Mindset	Growth Mindset
Challenges	Avoids challenges	Embraces challenges
Obstacles	Gives up easily	Persists in the face of setbacks
Effort	Sees effort as fruitless or worse	Sees effort as a path to mastery
Criticism	Ignores useful negative feedback	Seeks out feedback and learns from criticism
Success of others	Feels threatened by the success of others	Finds lessons and inspiration in the success of others

Understanding the difference between a fixed and a growth mindset is crucial to our fixing feedback movement. As you scan the comparisons between growth and fixed mindsets, it's vividly clear why: growth-mindset people embody the behaviors needed for better feedback experiences, while those individuals with a fixed mindset do not. Here's an idea that may seem a little less obvious: for feedback to serve as the catalyst to help us change, shift, grow, and improve, *both* parties, those offering and receiving, need to be operating from a growth mindset.

When I was a kid, my dad and I would head up to Big Mountain ski resort in Montana every winter weekend. My dad was the racing coach, which kept him busy all day, so I took lessons or skied with my friends. At the end of the day, as we were driving home, my father would always ask, "So, how many times did you fall today?" If I replied with zero, he'd shake his head disapprovingly and say, "If you're not falling, you're not learning." Being my dad, he knew me too well. He had a bead on my fixed view about my skiing. I'd skied since I was three and had decided I was good enough and as good as I was going to get. My dad's mindset wasn't fixed; he saw how much more opportunity I had to improve. He was right, of course, but I didn't see that at the time. I do now. That said, I'll admit I still don't like falling, especially now that I'm no longer a kid. However, my dad's words will sometimes pop into my head while I'm on the slopes, and when they do, I'll push myself just a little beyond my comfort zone.

GETTING YOUR GROWTH MINDSET ON

As is true of nearly all things in life, mindset is not a black and white proposition. All of us have a mixture of both growth and fixed mindsets, and the blend between the two evolves over time based on our experiences. We may have a fixed view related to one dimension of ourselves (*I can't do small talk*), and a growth mindset for others (*I don't know much about business strategy yet, but I'll bet I can get up to speed on it pretty quickly*). Our parsing of these self-perceptions is influenced by our life histories: what we were told by our parents, teachers, coaches, bosses, or friends, influential experiences, stereotypes we buy into, and more.

The good news is that we can shift ourselves and others from a predominantly fixed mindset to a predominantly growth mindset. However, as with the other brain shifts we've looked at, it takes focused effort and repetition.

TUNE IN

The important thing for those of us who want to grow and learn is to continually monitor our mindset. That requires us to tune into our inner voice. For example, when facing a new challenge, is your mind sending you fixed mindset messages? If so, evaluate your language and work toward switching it to a growth mindset, as in the following examples:

HOW WE SEE OURSELVES IN A FIXED OR GROWTH MINDSET

Fixed mindset	Growth mindset
I can't do this. I'm a failure.	I don't know how to do this yet. I wonder how I might learn more about it?
I've never been good at details.	Up until now, I haven't been good at details. I wonder what a quick web search on "how to get good at details" might reveal.
If I had Sara's people skills, I could close this deal.	I suspect some better people skills might help me close this deal. I think I'll talk with Sara to get her advice and see what I might learn.
I'm probably not up to this task.	I'm not feeling up to this task right now. But let's see how I feel after I spend a few minutes breaking the task down into subtasks.

Once you become more consistently aware of your own fixed mindset and more skilled at switching to a growth mindset, see if you can make the same shift in the way you think about others. If you often find yourself thinking and saying things that are rooted in judgment about people's potential, then you're likely operating from a fixed position. When we hold fixed mindsets about others' abilities to learn and grow, we unconsciously set limits. This may cause us to pass them over for challenging assignments that could expand their abilities and other professional learning opportunities. Here are a few examples of fixed ideas we might hold about others compared with how we might see them from more of a growth mindset:

HOW WE SEE OTHERS IN A FIXED OR GROWTH MINDSET

Fixed mindset	Growth mindset
Jim will never be good at this.	Jim's not good at this yet. But he's learned new things before and can do it again.
I'd have to give Mary that assignment because Jen simply couldn't handle it.	I'm pretty sure Mary could handle that assignment more easily than Jen. But it would be a good learning opportunity for Jen. I could offer to help get her started.
Tom will freak out if I'm honest with him about his work on that project.	I want to share some feedback with Tom about his work on that project. But I also need to emphasize my confidence in his ability to correct his mistakes and do better in the future.

Whether it concerns how we view our own abilities, limitations, and potential or those of others, thoughtfully tuning in to our inner voice helps us nip those fixed mindset patterns in the bud. Once we really hear the fixed mindset messages we're sending ourselves, we can make a habit of reshaping them into messages that spur growth instead of stunting it.

SHIFT FROM PROVE TO IMPROVE

When I painfully reflect on moments in my life when I've pegged the "jerk meter," I realize it is almost always when I'm trying to prove something to someone else or myself. You know what I'm talking about, right? Those times when we're busy being right, smart, talented, funny—whatever the aim, we're focused on that and not on being open and tuned into the needs and perspectives of others. I wish I could tell you that behavior is in my past now that I'm at a more wise, mature, and informed stage of life (or so I tell myself), but I'd be lying to you. What I can honestly tell you is that today I'm far more aware of when I slip into "prove" mode. Not only do I know it, but I'm also better at catching it and making an intentional switch to "improve" mode. When we flip the switch from prove to improve, we shift into a growth mindset and open ourselves up for so much more opportunity.

Because we humans long for connection and validation, I believe we'll always have to fight the tendency to pound our chests to prove our value and worthiness. That said, I trust that together we can rise above our egos and spend more of our time in improve mode. When receiving feedback, the greatest gift you can give yourself is to shift your mind into growth mode and openly consider what comes your way from the lens of how it can help you improve. Doing so saves you from performing the mental gymnastics that result from perceiving feedback as a threat to your identity. When offering feedback, we can use the idea of shifting from "prove" to "improve" to test our intent. In other words, are we extending this information to help the person improve or because we have something to prove? Switching from one to the other is an idea that can dramatically improve the quality of our feedback conversations.

PRACTICE MAKES PERFECT

Our troubled relationship with feedback has much to do with the way we humans are wired, and we have the power to change this relationship. Fear, negative leanings, and an often-distorted view of our place in the world are all part of what makes us human. But when left unexamined and unchecked, these triggers cripple our ability and willingness to pursue, offer, and accept feedback, even if it's perceived as being positive.

Fortunately, information is power, so recognizing these tendencies allows us to work toward freeing ourselves of their hold on us. And the more we practice doing so, the better we get. Every time we observe our fear, recognize it, and choose to keep it in check during a feedback conversation, we build new pathways in our brains that gradually replace the old, suboptimal choices (e.g., defend, deflect, cave in, or run away), overwriting bad habits with good.

In scientific terms, this is called neuroplasticity. Neuroplasticity is proven science that shows that we are continually shaping our brains through our everyday experiences. In simple terms, *we can use our minds to change our brains*. We're creating new pathways with each experience. Neural pathways become established by repetition in much the same way that hiking trails are gradually grooved into the forest floor by many feet treading the same path.

Creating new pathways with repetition and practice is a rather simple idea, but executing it takes determination, time, and plenty of practice. Hey, I never said that creating a movement would be easy!

FRESH START

CHAPTER 4

A FRESH START FOR FEEDBACK

WE'RE STARTING FRESH. We're launching our movement, all pulling in the same direction as we set our course to a new world of feedback. To ensure our success, we're letting go of the outmoded thinking and bad habits. To help us do that, we've armed ourselves with some scientific background on what's responsible for our dysfunctional relationship with old-school feedback.

And now we turn our focus forward. To the new. To creating a shared vision and a strong commitment to rebooting feedback. As we wipe the slate clean, we're going to chalk it in with a new definition for feedback, a common language, and new ideas and perspectives on what feedback looks like when it's good, impactful, and offered with the best of intentions.

A NEW DEFINITION OF FEEDBACK

If we look at the Oxford Dictionary definition of "feedback," we find this:

> **feedback** *(noun)*
> **1.** /ˈfēdˌbak/ Information about reactions to a product, a person's performance of a task, etc., which is used as a basis for improvement.

It's not horrible, but it's not great, and it's certainly not inspirational enough to usher in a new era of feedback. It doesn't say information shared to make you feel inadequate, labeled, or a disappointment, even though this is a common perception. It is, however, far too narrow and limited for our purposes, given the focus on performance, tasks, and improvement. And that word "reactions" feels a bit aggressive, doesn't it?

So let's set that old definition aside and found our movement on a new definition. A definition that will shift our perceptions, reactions, and engagement with feedback. A definition that is more specific and speaks to the outcomes and future we are seeking. Something like this:

> **feedback** *(noun)*
> **1.** /ˈfēdˌbak/ Clear and specific information that's sought or extended with the sole intention of helping individuals or groups improve, grow, or advance.

As with all definitions, the words have been carefully chosen. Let's break it down and get a deeper understanding of our new definition and its intended meaning:

CLEAR AND SPECIFIC. Shared information needs enough specificity to make it meaningful, providing clear understanding and inspiring action as appropriate.

SOUGHT OR EXTENDED. Feedback is as much about soliciting as it is about offering, with the aim of bringing information into a shared conversation.

SOLE INTENTION. If the feedback isn't intended to help individuals or teams thrive and grow, then why offer it or seek it? If it doesn't meet that sniff test, then don't fool yourself into thinking it's feedback.

IMPROVE. When a behavior, approach, action, attitude, or other factor is getting in the way, then the time might be right for some improvement feedback. Improvement-oriented feedback should help the individual know what to change and offer ideas for testing new approaches or techniques. It's best when offered with a perspective on what's getting in the way of better outcomes, and with a view to the future rather than dwelling in the past.

GROW. In our new definition we're applying growth in the broadest sense, recognizing that we can grow every day as we increase our awareness about who we are and how the world around us works, develop new talents, expand our networks, learn and test new approaches and ideas, and so much more. Growth is a never-ending journey, and when pursued with purpose it helps us become a better version of ourselves every day.

ADVANCE. While advancement requires growth, it also encompasses the idea of movement: stepping up to that next rung on the corporate ladder, taking on a bigger account, or accepting a broader role within the organization. We each hold our own views of growth and advancement and place differing levels of importance on each in our lives and careers. In our shared vision of the future we need to accept that we are all seeking growth, but also that we're all free to choose our own relationship with advancement. In short, some of us may choose to grow in place and leave the focus on advancement to others.

FEEDBACK: YES, THIS, NOT THAT!

When I'm trying to wrap my head around a new concept, I find it helpful to contrast what something is to what it isn't. Here's a little "is and isn't" comparison that should help flesh out our new definition of feedback:

WHAT FEEDBACK IS AND WHAT FEEDBACK ISN'T

Feedback is:	Feedback isn't:
A tool	A weapon
Communication	Accusation
Grounded in trust	Mired in suspicion
Observation offered with context	Judgment passed without context
Offered with the intent to help someone move toward something better	Offered with the intent to demonstrate your power
Thoughtful and concise	Scattered and verbose
Insights that draw upon shared experience	Stories intended to showcase your wisdom
Constructive	Destructive
An offering	A punishment
An invitation to self-reflection	A demand for self-blame
A way to help people	A way to fix people

ACCENTUATE THE POSITIVE

There's a phantom word that floats in front of feedback. Can you guess what it is? If I say, "I have some feedback for you," where does your mind go? To the negative, probably. I'll wager that what you heard me say is, "I've got some *negative* feedback for you." You wouldn't be alone if you did, since the majority of us are likely to mentally insert that dark word into what should be a harmless phrase.

How do we move past this almost instinctive impulse to assume that feedback is negative? We can start with our new definition, which doesn't qualify the nature of the feedback, and doesn't state whether the feedback is likely to be perceived as positive or negative by the recipient. That's on purpose.

At this point we need to clarify our thinking on positive and negative feedback. One common misconception is that the best way to really change a person's behavior or approach is to point out what they are doing wrong. Most of us share this belief, especially those of us who were raised in Western cultures. For years I thought this was true, and like many others I believed that sharing feedback the "right way" was a matter of summoning my courage to make some strong points about things that needed "fixing."

Boy, was I wrong. And if you still believe negative feedback is the most powerful option in your feedback playbook, then I'm afraid you're wrong, too. (Yikes, there's a little negative feedback for you!) Negative feedback ("improvement feedback" will be the preferred term in our new movement) does serve an important function: it may be vital when something or someone is really going off the rails. I'm talking about when the actions or behaviors of the individual or group is causing serious concern for their future or significantly impacting those around them. If you're witnessing someone about to go off the high dive into an empty pool, then by all means, stop them. Call it out, discuss it, keep your focus on the impacts, and present your case without judgment. Take it on because you care, not to make a power play or demonstrate how right you are.

As you work side by side with your colleagues, your bosses, and your teams, how often are the people around you that far off track? Not that often. So devote your energy and focus to delivering positive feedback—it's where you'll have the most power and influence, by far. Positive feedback tells people to keep doing the good stuff, do it even more frequently, do it well, and hone their strengths and contributions. Positive feedback is inspirational; it elevates us and gives us the impetus to try harder. It creates focused energy, and focused energy drives improvement, growth, better outcomes, and greater impact.

Positive feedback is always recognition, but recognition is not always positive feedback.

POSITIVE FEEDBACK VERSUS RECOGNITION

While we're building clarity on our definitions of feedback, let's also take the time to differentiate positive feedback from recognition. If we recognize an individual with a general statement like "I really like working with you," then we've said something kind and encouraging. It's a great form of recognition, and we should say those things often. But that statement is positively not positive feedback. Why? It's not specific. It's not actionable. It doesn't tell that person why you like working with them or what elements of your collaboration you value most. Alternatively, if you say, "I really like working with you. I've noticed how your ability to take my ideas and advance them really impacts the quality of the marketing ideas we're bringing back to the team," that's both positive feedback *and* recognition. It's communicating both what you value and how it's impacting results.

My advice is to do more of each. Take the time to recognize those around you, and also think about where you can provide specific and actionable positive feedback. Those you work with will thank you for the effort—on both fronts.

SEEKERS, RECEIVERS, AND EXTENDERS

Our fresh start calls for not only a new definition of feedback but also a shared language that clarifies the different players in the process of feedback. At any given time, we may find ourselves playing any one of three roles in a feedback conversation: Seeker, Receiver, and Extender.

While this may seem pretty straightforward, it's important that we agree on common definitions for each of these roles:

Seekers
Individuals who proactively request feedback from others with the intention of self-development or growth

RECEIVERS
Recipients of feedback— sought or unsought, wanted or unwanted

EXTENDERS
Those who give feedback to others, either proactively or by request

Given that we all switch from Seeker to Receiver to Extender so frequently, we've devoted a full chapter to each of these roles to examine the unique challenges and fixes associated with them. But first, let's talk about how we lay the foundation that our success and effectiveness in any of these three roles depend on.

FOUNDATIONS

CHAPTER 5

THE FOUNDATIONS OF FIXING FEEDBACK

THE POWER OF TRUST

Trust, trust, trust: It's the vital ingredient that makes feedback work.

If you receive feedback from someone you don't trust or don't have at least a semblance of a connection with, it's likely to go straight into the mental round file (even if it's positive). If you share an insight with someone who doesn't trust you, know you, or share your values, you might rev up the "fight, flight, or freeze" response in them. Trust greases the feedback gears, allowing information to flow without friction. Without trust, we simply don't allow ourselves to experience the growth, improvement, and advancement impacts we seek.

Trust isn't handed out like Halloween candy; it's a valuable commodity that doesn't come cheap. It's built one interaction at a time, over time. It's not driven by a single event but by a collection of moments that matter and experiences that knit us together. It's hard to earn and it's easy to lose. And when it comes to building genuine trust, the feeling has to be mutual.

To build trust, we need a track record of engaging in feedback conversations that help and don't hurt. Feedback in trusting conversations creates a reinforcing loop, and the trajectory can be either positive or negative. Applying good feedback practices and avoiding those that we know will set off the alarm bells in the fear center are vital to growing trust. Trust allows us to collectively move forward in productive, growth-oriented ways.

We can't force anyone to trust us, but there are sound actions each of us can take that make it easier for others to learn to trust us. Here are a few of the basics.

BE HUMAN. When we get wrapped up in our titles, positions, and expectations, it's easy to forget to simply be human. And what does it mean to be human?

- Made a mistake? Admit it!
- Be authentic to who you are. Let your values show.
- Get personal. It's okay to share your thoughts and feelings. Having the courage to specifically name or identify our emotions helps us connect more easily with one another, inside and outside of work.
- Don't take yourself too seriously. Seriously!

DO WHAT YOU SAY YOU'LL DO. No one will trust you if you don't stick to the commitments you've made and deal with people and situations with honesty.

- If you make a promise, keep it. If you've overcommitted, acknowledge it.
- Don't offer things you can't deliver.
- Be consistent: reliability is key.
- Don't lie, conceal, exaggerate, or blow smoke.

BE KIND. Trust can only thrive in an environment of safety. If you're unpredictable, trust will be shattered by fear. Trust comes when we:

- Encourage others.

- Speak with kindness, eliminating criticism, defensiveness, and blame from our conversations.
- Are there when we're needed.
- Value the needs of others as much as our own.

CONNECT. Trust requires good connections, and good connections require an investment in time and effort. This means we:

- Spend focused time with others and are present when doing so.
- Always seek the win-win.
- Allow for collaboration and let go of control.
- Truly consider another's viewpoint and ideas without judgment.

CONNECT FIRST

Connections drive trust, and trust drives feedback, so fixing feedback must start with building human connections. Through these moments of connection, we build relationships. From there, trust is built, and where there's trust, there's a healthy environment for great feedback. There's no shortcut. It takes time, but it's time well spent.

Trust helps quell the primitive brain's "fight, flight, or freeze" urge by sending messages like:

- This is a friend, not a foe, so I don't need to fight.
- This person has my best interests in mind and is not likely trying to harm me, so I don't need to flee.
- I can stick my neck out, take a risk, and share my thoughts, feelings, and faults. I don't need to freeze or appease.

Homo sapiens is a profoundly social species. Our most joyful moments come from closeness with others, while our saddest often stem from social isolation, losing a connection, or a lack of belonging. (Remember, the threat of not belonging is the key driver behind our fear of feedback.) As we spend time at work connecting with people we grow to feel at ease with, we develop a strong individual and collective sense of well-being, trust, and safety. And when those factors are present, we're far more likely to take risks, be innovative, and go the extra mile when necessary. And guess what else happens when we connect with and trust one another? We're also far more likely to seek, extend, and receive feedback.

We've set the starting point for building our feedback movement: connecting with those who work with us every day. That's not just our boss and the people who report to us but also our peers, our internal customers, our external customers, and the others we collaborate with to get work done. All of these people have feedback for you that can help you grow, improve, and advance. And I'll bet you have a few helpful ideas for them, too.

THE GOTTMAN 5:1

Five to one. Remember that ratio! It's insightful. It's telling. It's a core foundational concept for developing and sustaining trusted connections and relationships.

Our team at PeopleFirm is tuned in to the work of Dr. John Gottman, a renowned therapist in the field of marriage stability and divorce prediction. With more than 40 years of research and as many books to his name, Dr. Gottman exerts a powerful influence on our work in leadership, team dynamics, and, yes, feedback.

In tandem with his research partner, Robert Levenson, Dr. Gottman conducted longitudinal studies of couples they tracked for nine years.[1] Their findings are striking. Here's the crux of what they learned:

- Couples who flourished engaged differently than those who did not.
- "The difference between happy and unhappy couples is the balance between positive and negative interactions during conflict."[2]

- Stable and happy marriages had five (or more) positive interactions for every negative interaction (the 5:1 ratio).
- In the end, they were able to predict divorce in *more than 90 percent* of the couples who were unable to achieve this ratio.

If engagement and positive interaction exert such a profound influence on marriage stability, then perhaps their learnings are translatable to workplace relationships as well.

Five to one: what does that look like in practice? Well, it doesn't mean dreaming up five positive yet insincere things to say about someone in order to sugarcoat a particularly bitter feedback pill. What it does mean is increasing the ratio (yes, up to five to one) of positive *connections* with one another. These interactions don't need to be related to feedback. A connection may be participating in a social event, asking how someone's doing and really listening, sharing recognition or gratitude, or working together on a tough challenge. It can be as simple as lending an ear to a colleague who's having a rough day, or positively challenging another's point of view. In essence, it can be anything that fortifies trust. This may not sound that difficult, but most of us struggle to find time and energy for these moments of connection in the midst of our frantic, overscheduled daily routines. We have to actively seek those moments of genuine interest, empathy, and relatability where we are putting someone else's needs first. For our movement to be a success, this hard (yet not hard) work must happen throughout the day, every day.

Trust, connections, and relationships that have staying power and that feel safe are our foundations for our new brand of feedback. The Gottman 5:1 ratio provides a powerful yet simple reminder of how we can achieve those goals.

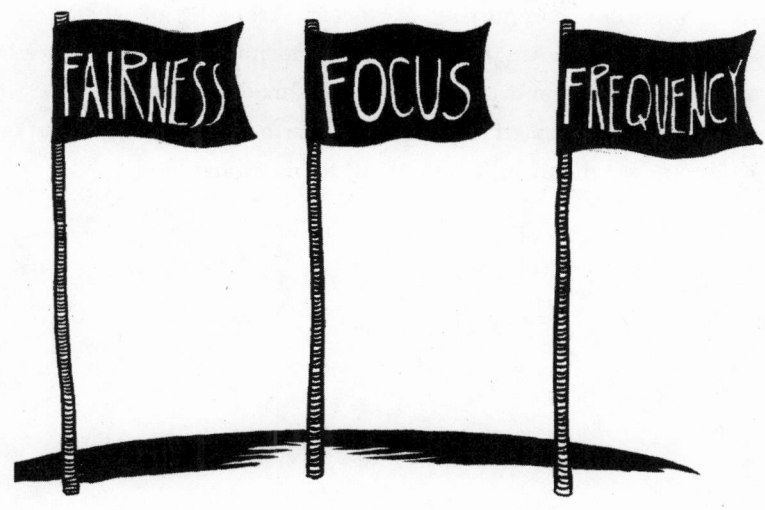

THE THREE FOUNDATIONAL Fs
OF FEEDBACK: FAIRNESS, FOCUS,
AND FREQUENCY

Every successful movement needs a call to action, a motto that inspires its followers and keeps them true to their mission. The French Revolution had "Liberté, Egalité, Fraternité." We're launching our movement under the banner of "Fairness, Focus, and Frequency," and we'll fly the flag of the three Fs high and proud.

In the sections that follow, we'll demonstrate that every great feedback experience is anchored in fairness, focus, and frequency. When combined, these three Fs create a safe environment for Seekers, Extenders, and Receivers of feedback to request, share, digest, and explore ideas and recommendations that can help each of them grow. There's plenty of data to back this up, including a 2002 Corporate Leadership study of more than 19,000 employees that found the strongest lever of increased performance was the fairness and accuracy of a manager's descriptive feedback. Frequently observing direct reports and reporting on specific examples of what they saw without evaluating it increased performance by as much as 39 percent.[3] As we move forward, these three elements will be essential to every impactful feedback scenario we'll explore, so let's make sure we understand each of our foundational Fs.

Fairness

The first fabulous F we'll explore is fairness. "It's just not fair!" is the universal lament of angry children learning to cope with the sense that they're being treated unjustly. The thing is, that lament still rings in our heads when we step into our work lives. We might use more grown-up words and our "inside voices" to register our complaint, but the resentment and frustration triggered by a perceived lack of fairness still run deep.

Fairness is locked arm in arm with trust, so it's hard to overstate its role in setting the scene for successful feedback. When present, fairness binds relationships; when absent or insufficient, it can break or damage them. If our relationships are tainted by a perceived lack of fairness, then feedback simply won't work. When trust and fairness are absent, because either the feedback itself or its Extender seems unfair or biased, the Receiver retreats into protection mode.

Our primitive mind tells us to flee the scene in order to protect what we hold dear, rejecting what could be good, valuable information. On the other hand, when we engage in a feedback conversation that is perceived as fair and trustworthy, the "threat state" red alert fails to activate. You are in the right frame of mind to actually settle in and listen, engaging in the conversation with your wise brain in control. Fair feedback reinforced again and again becomes almost as natural to you as breathing. We deepen our connection with others we are in feedback conversations with, and we come away from the interaction with information that has the potential to help us grow, develop, and reach for our potential.

One of the challenges in operating with fairness is the unavoidable effect cognitive bias has on every one of us.[4] Regardless of whether you're offering or accepting feedback, your engagement in the exchange is unavoidably influenced by your own biases. Simply put, biases are the shortcuts we use when making judgments and predictions. In a world where we are faced with thousands of choices every day, bias is a survival instinct that helps the human brain make rapid choices.

When we hear the word "bias," our thoughts automatically turn to racial prejudice or political bias. While racial, religious, sexual, and other similar prejudices are bias at its worst, it's vital we recognize that a smorgasbord of cognitive biases influences our views and drives faulty thinking for all of us. We've already discussed negativity bias and how it often influences how we receive feedback. Confirmation bias, another dangerous influence on feedback, leads us to look for evidence that supports or confirms our current point of view and helps us discount or ignore evidence that contradicts our opinion. Other more commonly known biases include recency bias, the halo effect, positivity bias, and so many more. One of my new favorites is bias blind spot, the tendency to see oneself as less biased than other people. In fact, as you scan the unofficial list of almost

200 cognitive biases on Wikipedia, it's not hard to see how a number of these biases can negatively influence feedback fairness.

Think you can escape the effects of bias? Think again. Even the most well-intended among us are incapable of fully rising above their biases. So, if we're all guilty of dozens of forms of bias, how in the world do we achieve fairness? Good question. We'll continue to ponder how to tackle this challenge a little later, but for now let's leave it at this:

- The first step is accepting that we are biased and continuing to work to enhance our awareness and understanding of how our biases influence our thinking.
- If we extend (and receive) feedback without judgment, we're operating in far safer waters.
- We can minimize the effects of bias when feedback is an exploratory conversation—an open and honest exchange of what we believe we've witnessed or experienced.
- Finally, the more we look outside of ourselves and invite others into the conversation, the better off we'll all be. In other words, seeking multiple sources can be one of our best weapons against the brain's natural bias wiring.

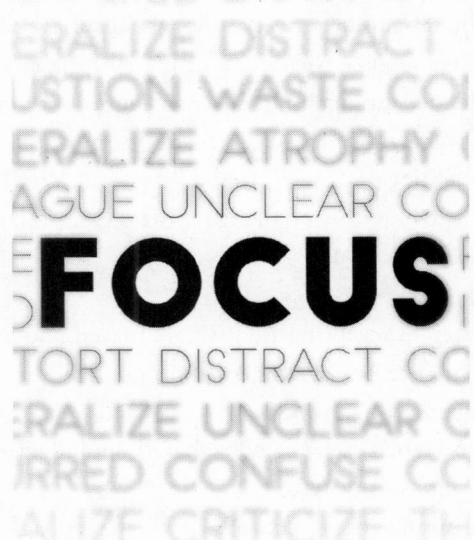

Focus

The second vital F in feedback is focus. Focus is about making feedback specific, targeted, and brief. It's a big idea delivered in small bites. Too much is too much, so get to the damn point or your feedback partner's brain will shut down and shut you out.

I like to think of focused feedback as snacking on positivity and possibilities, not gorging on performance reviews and barely digestible diatribe. As my favorite font of wisdom, author Seth Godin, says, "Snacking is learning." Well, feedback is learning, too, and it's best when it comes in a concentrated form—a concise, specific, and actionable morsel of information. And remember that focus applies to both planned and spontaneous feedback. Dishing out bite-sized portions of off-the-cuff gratitude, recognition, direction, or coaching can move the performance needle much more effectively than hours of training sessions, development seminars, or dismal laundry lists of your rights and wrongs from the past year.

Frequency

If fairness and focus provide the fuel for our feedback engine, then our third F, frequency, is the accelerator. Connecting frequently speaks volumes. It says, "I'm paying attention, what you do is important and notable, and you are a priority." That alone creates plenty of goodwill, without even factoring in the additional positive impact of knowledge sharing and connection building that can result from these moments. In the Corporate Leadership study mentioned earlier, performance increased by 30 percent when managers were knowledgeable about their direct reports' performance. In the realm of performance increases, those are some big numbers!

The secret sauce of frequency is its informal and spontaneous nature. A quick observation, delivered without pomp and circumstance, will have more impact than infrequent, formal conversations. Organizations all over the globe are seeing bottom-line performance improvement as they ditch the dreaded and ineffective annual performance review in favor of purposeful collaboration through frequent and consistent feedback.

Just how frequent is "frequent"? Research suggests a minimal pacing of every two weeks for informal feedback is best. If it's part of your daily routine, then the effect will be even greater. Is it worth the time? Absolutely. Frequency increases the quality of our relationships and accelerates our learning, and it's an easy and effective way to deepen neural pathways to improve feedback of all kinds.

THE FINE ART OF NOTICING

Laura and I hope that if there's only one practice you take away from this content, it's that you'll unclutter your mind of all the training sessions, lectures, articles, and struggles to expose your bias about feedback and put your energy into one thing: *noticing*. The shift away from formal performance appraisals or evaluations to a more present and accessible practice of noticing is so important to our movement that we've declared it an art form: the Fine Art of Noticing (FAN).

FAN, carried out under the banner of "Fairness, Focus, and Frequency," is potent stuff. Noticing is observing without judgment. When we notice ourselves, other people, or behaviors without judgment, we observe things as they are, without attaching emotion. Dictionary.com provides this simple definition of the word observe: "to regard with attention, especially so as to see or learn something." Like other ideas that have the power to change the world, it's surprisingly uncomplicated, but when artfully executed, it can transform feedback. We recognize that FAN, like any other craft, takes practice. We test, we learn, we get better, and we build new neural pathways that make noticing, not judging, second nature, like breathing.

We propose 10 commitments to help us grow our skills in "noticing":

F.A.N.
(The Fine Art of Noticing)
10 Commitments

1. We commit to the idea that noticing is about helping others and ourselves understand, learn, and grow.

2. We notice without judgment, sharing clear and factual insights.

3. We rely on firsthand observation, not hearsay or assumptions.

4. We focus on the moment, the present, the here and now.

5. We fully embrace fairness, focus, and frequency in our craft.

6. We accept that noticing is not about status, power, or position.

7. We acknowledge that noticing applies both to ourselves and to others.

8. We act as witness to the progress around us, we don't wait for perfection.

9. We are tuned in and paying attention - always.

10. We consider the future, the possibilities. "How can my noticing help us see and learn together?"

Just as important as understanding what it means to embrace the Fine Art of Noticing is to recognize the legacy of feedback and the practices we're letting go of. When we engage in FAN we're no longer banking feedback for long, awkward sit-downs where we dredge up the muck accumulated during the last six months. We're letting go of lists: the good and the bad, the strengths and the weaknesses, the ups and the downs. We're pulling the plug on ratings, rankings, and comparisons. We're axing the anonymous 360 surveys. We're consciously stepping away from triangulation and hallway gossip. (Triangulation is a manipulation tactic where one person will not communicate directly with another person, instead using a third person to relay communication to the second, thus forming a triangle.) We're rejecting the power imbalance that too often exists among Seekers, Extenders, and Receivers of feedback. We're saying goodbye to traditions, old-school thinking, and practices that may have had all the best intentions, but which have failed to create the environment of safety and trust in which people can flourish.

That's a lot of baggage to leave behind. You may find that it makes you a little uncomfortable to let those ideas and practices go, given the fact that most of us grew up in a world that honored and demanded some, if not all, of them. But as leaders of the feedback movement, we need to have the courage to be the first to walk away from the familiar and embrace new and better habits and practices.

CONNECT: A SIMPLE CONVERSATION GUIDE

It's tough pulling all these concepts together. I get it. Keeping the commitments to the Fine Art of Noticing, including fairness, focus, and frequency, takes work. So does striving to keep our biases in check, thinking of the right things to say, when to say them, and initiating a focused and comprehensible conversation with a delivery that is authentic, unscripted, and genuine. Sheesh, who wouldn't toss the whole feedback shebang out the door and just avoid it altogether? Some of my most senior coaching clients struggle with this when we work together to prepare for courageous feedback conversations. In fact, these struggles inspired the creation of this simple conversation guide we call CONNECT. It's designed to help you script and prepare for feedback connections of all varieties. While originally designed for those who are extending feedback, we find this model helpful to frame up and plan any feedback conversation. My Seeker and Receiver clients tell me it's useful when a less skilled Extender pops up with some feedback, since it helps them enter the conversation and stems that urge to fight, flee, freeze, or appease.

Laura

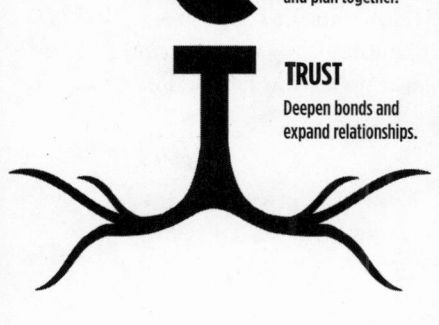

CONTEXT

Be clear about the situation.

- Ask first.
- Share your intention.
- Provide clarity on your topic.
- Describe the situation or circumstances; be specific.

ONE THING

Focus on the most important thing you want to discuss.

- Focus feedback on one bite (i.e., one thing).
- Hone in on what's most important.
- Avoid the "pile-on."
- Don't serve up a sh•t sandwich.

NOTICE

Factually describe what you observed.

- Provide clear details as you describe the specific behaviors or situation you observed or participated in.
- Notice without attributing motive or judgment; no blame or shame.

NO G.R.I.T.

Avoid Gossip, Rumor, Inuendo, or Triangulation.

- Speak to what you know. No evaluation. No assumptions.
- Trust that everyone has best intentions.

EFFECT

Share the resulting impact.

- Describe the effect or impact on both the Receiver and others (you, peers, company, customers).
- Share your thoughts and emotions.
- Describe the future behavior or situation without demanding or demeaning.

CONVERSATION

Talk, test, explore, learn, and plan together.

- Talk face to face. Sit down together or, at minimum, video chat.
- Shift from knower to learner.
- Listen to and strive to understand each other's point of view.
- Ask questions that expand the conversation.
- Don't rush to act.

TRUST

Deepen bonds and expand relationships.

- Keep the connection going by planning your next conversation.
- Cocreate next steps and agree to a commitment.
- Recognize that with each positive connection you're strengthening the relationship.
- Trusted feedback gets easier and more natural with time and practice.

CONNECT EXAMPLE 1:
APRIL EXTENDS POSITIVE FEEDBACK TO MANUEL

CONTEXT	
"Manuel, I'd like to share some great stuff I've heard from the client about your work this week. Is this a good time to chat?"	✓ Manuel knows April is offering positive feedback. ✓ April asks in advance if the time is right.

ONE THING	
"This is about the illustrations you've been working on for the new training materials."	✓ The focus is clearly identified as the illustrations for the new training materials.

NOTICE	
"The last six full-page illustrations you created were rated as 'customer delighters' in the recent customer satisfaction survey. They particularly liked your 'font as illustration.'"	✓ The behavior or skill (creating the illustrations) is called out. ✓ April factually describes what the client liked. ✓ Specific details are communicated about the illustration the customer rated highly.

NO G.R.I.T.	
"You found a unique way to meet all the customer specs and add a bit of your personal flair."	✓ April recognizes Manuel's great work without resorting to contrasting it or comparing it with the work of others.

EFFECT

"Your approach led to a top rating, which is great to have as a testimonial on the company website. Excellent performance like this gets us more work—the kind of work I know you are passionate about. It makes me proud to see you get this kind of recognition. I hope you're pleased as well."

✓ April shares the positive present and future impacts of Manuel's work.
✓ The future benefit to Manuel is made clear when April mentions that his great performance increases the potential for more of the work he's passionate about.
✓ April shares her emotions relating to Manuel's positive feedback, which strengthens their connection.

CONVERSATION

April: "Well done! How do you feel about this?"
Manuel: "Thank you, April! I feel great being part of the team that got this done. Let me know if you have any other specifics. I'm interested to see if the other drawings hit the mark, or if I should tweak them. I'd love to work on more projects like this. Let me know how I can raise my hand for another client assignment when it comes up."

✓ April offers Manuel the opportunity to respond to the feedback.
✓ Manuel lets April know that he's engaged in growth-minded, future-focused thinking.

TRUST

Trust and connection grow when Manuel makes it clear to April that the feedback has inspired him to tune in to more opportunities to do work he loves and excels at.

CONNECT EXAMPLE 2: MAX EXTENDS IMPROVEMENT FEEDBACK TO CHARLENE

CONTEXT	
"Charlene, I'd like some time with you to talk about the ship-and-load schedule for Thursday. I understand we're behind, and some deadlines may have been missed. Would you be willing to meet at four tomorrow afternoon so I can learn more?"	✓ Max asks in advance to speak to Charlene. ✓ The subject (the ship-and-load schedule) and the issue (missed deadlines) are clearly stated.

ONE THING	
"I understand we're behind and some deadlines may have been missed."	✓ The missed deadline is the one thing. ✓ Max is clear so Charlene doesn't need to get anxious wondering what he wants to talk about.

NOTICE	
"The tracking report detail shows that the ship-and-load schedule was off by four hours on Thursday, and that stall came from our group. Can you please confirm my understanding?" "I recall that you and I had an agreement to signal each other early if we were going to miss a deadline."	✓ These are the facts as Max understands them now. He checks for clarity just in case. ✓ Judgment might have looked like: "You really dropped the ball on this. I thought we had an agreement."

EFFECT

"If I don't know we've missed the deadline, I can't get ahead of it. As a result, we collectively take the hit to our on-time metric and we pay · late penalties. It's frustrating for me, and I assume for you too, knowing your goal of being the top on-time unit in the plant. Let's talk about how we can get there together."

✓ The effect is noted as both the hit to the on-time metric and the penalty fees.

✓ Without belaboring the problem, Max quickly pivots to illustrate the desired future state (being the top on-time unit in the plant).

CONVERSATION

Max: "Can you tell me what happened and how we can make sure we don't have a miss like this again?"

Charlene: "I knew I was cutting it close, and then a last-minute snafu caused an unexpected delay which put us really behind. I'm sorry, Max. In hindsight, I realize I should have let you know the risk I was taking sooner."

✓ When Charlene feels free to share what was going on in her head, she can get to the root of the issue.

✓ When Charlene helps cocreate the next steps, she is more likely to be motivated to make the change needed to deliver better results next time.

TRUST

Together they make a plan for an early warning signal if a deadline is in jeopardy in the future. Charlene feels comfortable in the conversation, yet remains accountable for the mistake. Max chose to address the hard issue but not shame Charlene, so she is more likely to ask for what she needs next time. Trust and connection have been furthered.

Seekers

INDIVIDUALS WHO PROACTIVELY SEEK FEEDBACK FROM OTHERS WITH THE INTENTION OF SELF-DEVELOPMENT OR GROWTH

CHAPTER 6

SEEKING FEEDBACK

AS WE GROW OUR MOVEMENT to inspire great feedback practices, we're first enlisting Seekers. After all, it's the most important role any of us can play in fixing feedback. Why? Because the movement starts within. With ourselves. Seeking, not knowing. Learning, not always telling.

Research tells us that organizations that shift from giving feedback to asking for it drive performance improvement, growth mindset, effective decision making, and stronger, more resilient teams.[1]

The benefits of being a Seeker are many:

- It's the ultimate trust generator. Seeking demonstrates humility and shows you value the perspectives of others.
- People who ask for feedback feel greater autonomy and control.
- When you're seeking, you're more likely to act on the feedback.
- Asking means you get to focus on the information you need to meet your goals.
- As the Seeker, you choose the time and the place, ensuring that you'll be in the right mindset for the conversation.

- Seeking first is the best way to start a movement. (Here's your chance to go first if you're a leader or manager!)

As Seeker, your role is to build connections with others and nurture those trusted relationships to help you learn and grow. This is your course to set. Perhaps your goal is to build a skill in a new discipline. If so, then it makes sense to target others who have the skill you want and request their insights. You might ask, "What's the best way to get started? What experiences helped you build your capabilities? Am I on the right track so far?"

You may be seeking something deeper. Perhaps you've recognized that you're struggling with certain work relationships. In this case, you may be asking others to reflect on and share how they're seeing you show up, if there are behaviors they're observing that you may not be aware of, or what they've experienced personally when collaborating with you. In any of these scenarios, the key is that you're doing the asking, so you'll focus the discussion and then decide what you'll do with the information you receive. All in all, that's a powerful place to be!

CREATE CONNECTIONS

At this point you're well versed in the concept that connections are vital to making feedback work. As a Seeker, connections are vital to the quality of the feedback you'll harvest and the strength of the relationships you will form.

Multiple studies have shown that people dislike giving feedback just as much as, if not more than, receiving it. So, while you may think the Extender is always in the driver's seat, your request for feedback may actually ignite fear in them. Three easy steps can prevent that from happening:

1. Build a relationship before you go seeking. Having a platform from which you're making the request is key.
2. Provide context. Tell them why you're asking and why their insights are important to you.
3. Use techniques that help them feel prepared. I'm talking about focused requests based on what they are noticing.

Once you've created a relationship and you've helped those you're seeking insights from understand your expectations, they're far more likely to feel safe and comfortable in the Extender role you've asked them to play. Seeking first may be the most effective catalyst for creating connections and building sustainable, trusted relationships. Seek and you shall find!

LEADERS GO FIRST

Are you a leader? Maybe your title is CEO, VP, or director, or maybe it's team lead or project manager. Perhaps you have a thousand people working under you, or just one or two. Regardless of your span of control or your title, if you're leading in *any* capacity, you need to know what I'm about to tell you.

Thirty years of research has identified the top factor in driving change: leadership. Change happens when leaders are engaged and committed. It often fails when they are not. Heeding this insight, we know that to change the culture of an organization and the actions and habits of a group of people, leaders need to be committed to the change *and* get out front to blaze the trail.

Leading doesn't mean sending a perfunctory email or adding a slide to the deck for the annual meeting to let folks know you're all "rah-rah" about feedback. Leading means embracing and modeling the new habits, new behaviors, and new culture you're working to create. Simply said, leaders need to walk the talk. This shouldn't be taken lightly—it's a commitment. Once you sign up to lead, your task is to stay the course. Now, we all have our off days, but the key to being a successful leader is to seek feedback from others so you can be aware of them when you might not recognize them yourself, acknowledge them honestly when they happen (which builds credibility in your team's eyes), and get back on track quickly once you know that you've tripped up. In short, get some feedback on how you are approaching feedback.

The success of this movement depends heavily on placing the emphasis and focus on the Seeker. We want people to seek first, and we want Seekers to take control. Creating an environment where seeking is commonplace will be the catalyst for true and sustainable culture change.

To get there we need leaders to, well, lead. Be the first in your organization to consistently ask for feedback. Openly share with others what you're up to, invite them to share their perspectives, and encourage them to become fellow Seekers. Not only will this activity give impetus to the movement we're trying to create, it will also send a strong signal about your leadership style. And the ultimate bonus is how much you'll benefit and grow from the information you'll glean.

Here are just a few reasons for leaders to begin seeking:

- You'll build new trusted connections with those around you and deepen existing ones.
- You'll lessen the fear in others when you ask them to help you.
- You'll reinforce the idea that none of us is perfect, and that it's okay for you and everyone on your team to have some flaws and make some mistakes now and then.
- You'll set a precedent that your people can come to you to share both the good and the bad, which will be liberating for them and enlightening for you.
- You'll boost your own leadership game. (Remember the finding in the Folkman and Zenger study I referenced way back in chapter 2 that leaders who ranked in the top 10 percent for asking for feedback also ranked at the top for overall leadership?)

KNOW YOUR FEEDBACK SELF

When we feel safe, we have better conversations. This is true for both Seekers and Extenders. In an atmosphere of safety, Seekers will be more transparent and authentic, and Extenders are more likely to share openly. Take a little time to consider what's important to you and what elements are key to your own feeling of safety. Capture your thoughts on our simple Feedback Guide template, and then share it with those you're seeking insights from so they feel comfortable about what you're asking of them. Update your Feedback Guide as you learn more about your true feedback self and remember to keep sharing it with those you invite into your feedback ecosystem.

MY FEEDBACK GUIDE

THESE DAYS I'M PASSIONATE ABOUT:	
ONE THING I'M WORKING ON:	
IF YOU HAVE FEEDBACK FOR ME, ONE SUGGESTION TO HELP IT STICK:	
I HAVE A HARD TIME WITH FEEDBACK WHEN:	
I FEEL APPRECIATED WHEN:	
ONE LAST THING YOU SHOULD KNOW:	

HITTING RESET: CHANGE YOUR ROLE

If you're a "my way or the highway" type—one who's always quick with harsh judgments and frank opinions—then imagine how pleasantly surprised your colleagues will be when you approach them with humility and sincerity to ask for their honest input on your performance. It's likely you'll need to lay a little groundwork to earn trust and signal that your metamorphosis into a Seeker is authentic. You can do this by acknowledging your past shortcomings and by detailing the work you're doing to shift how people experience you. Don't push too hard, though. Start small and enlist them to let you know when you stray from your path to better listening and sharing. Your trust in them will provide them the security to trust in you.

KICK SOME ASK

Seekers, you need to be bold and get out there to *kick some ask*. By doing so you'll be taking the reins of this feedback movement and leading it where it needs to go. As you do so, remember these four tips:

ASK IN ADVANCE. Asking in advance is the most effective way to get what you seek. It clarifies for the Extender the information you're seeking, and it allows them time to consider and prepare their answer. Giving them advance notice avoids putting them in the awkward position of feeling on the spot, and it will usually improve the quality of the feedback they provide.

GIVE THEM PERMISSION. When you ask for feedback, you give those generous Extenders the permission to be frank and honest. Remember, we humans don't like giving feedback, but when permission is offered, we can steer clear of fear and feel more comfortable and confident extending truth. By giving them permission, you're contracting with them psychologically. You're offering them the freedom to speak candidly while providing detail on what kind of feedback you're seeking and why. With the right tone and clear expectations set in advance, your time together can be spent mining for truth and building trust.

ASK THEM TO START NOTICING. If you're working on improvement in a key area, at a specific skill, or in specific situations, ask others to turn on their noticing on your behalf. Let them know the nature of the feedback you're looking for and when you'll be looping back to see what they observed. Ask them to provide, as much as possible, a descriptive view of what they noticed.

MAKE THE CHOICE. If fairness, focus, and frequency were involved, you are now holding a valuable nugget of feedback to process. You have the right to choose what happens next. Your power lies in choosing.

A final word on seeking: I want to reinforce that asking for feedback gets you ahead of your own "triggers." It not only gives the Extender time to prepare, it also helps you take control and avoid that problematic state of managing the things that tend to push your emotional buttons. It's not easy to ask, but when we shift our mindset from "prove" to "improve" and start seeking feedback from those who witness us day in and day out, we can fundamentally change our lives for the better.

FOCUS YOUR ASK

Focusing the conversation on what will be most useful to you is Job One for Seekers. There are two key reasons why a focused ask should be your seeking priority:

- Research indicates that we are likely to stimulate a fear response in a potential Extender when we hit them with a broad ask like "How am I doing?" The best means for lowering their stress is to request feedback that's specific and focused, such as, "When I present to the IT team today, could you pay attention to how much eye contact I'm making? I've also been working on keeping my feet planted and not walking around or pacing, so monitor that as well, please. I think my content will connect more if I improve in those areas."
- A focused ask allows you to put your energy, and that of the Extender, into something that is valuable and relevant to you. Your targeted ask allows you to take control and guide the direction of the feedback. You get what you need. The Extender gets to respond to a clearly defined request. You don't have to filter through a laundry list of offerings, and the Extender isn't wasting time giving you advice on something you couldn't care less about. It's a win-win!

While focusing your feedback ask is a priority, you may also consider taking a leap of faith and ask a trusted colleague to let you know about any blind spots they've noticed. Maybe they've witnessed you drop the ball on listening recently or spread yourself too thin when a tight deadline on a certain project deserves your undivided attention. You'll get the double benefit of hearing feedback about something that's high on the list of skills you value, and something that you might not be seeing.

Remember that asking for focused feedback is key to building our movement. You'll serve as a model to those around you, who will surely be inspired to seek feedback for themselves.

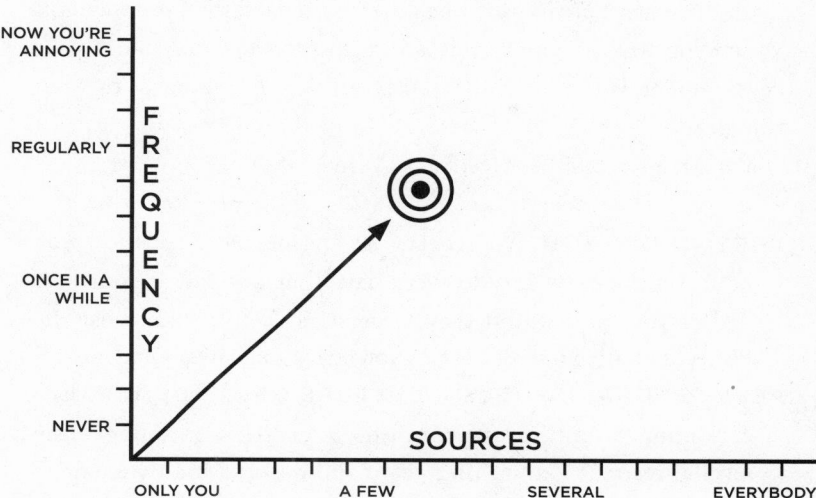

MORE SOURCES = BETTER LEARNING

The more sources of feedback you enlist, the more you'll increase the learnings and insights you can gather. Additionally, getting feedback from a cross-section of people makes it more likely that you'll get a truer picture of your performance than if you're relying only on the observations of one coworker. If you're working on a problem, trying to improve your game, tackling that next level on the competency ladder, or striving to be a better leader, then gathering perspectives from numerous angles will increase the fairness and accuracy of the feedback that you take in.

Of course, I'm not talking about running around yelling, "Tell me what to do! Tell me what to do!" I'm talking about a good, solid, focused ask from multiple sources (ideally, one that's made in advance). Your contributors should include those who have challenged you to think differently in the past, or those who've been critical of your work from time to time. When you step out of your safety zone in terms of whom you seek out, you might learn that what you bring to the table has more impact (or a different impact) than you thought. When you welcome more voices into the conversation about your development, you're likely to be surprised, often pleasantly, by what you glean.

I'm a huge fan of peer feedback. Why?

THEY KNOW YOU. Your peers are the people who know you best. They're by your side every day. They see you at your best and at your worst, and they understand better than most the kinds of challenges you face as you strive to grow and advance.

PEER FEEDBACK FUELS A CULTURE OF FEEDBACK. Encouraging a culture of peer-to-peer feedback encourages the level of recognition within a team and builds a highly energizing work environment that leads to greater engagement and productivity. A recent Globoforce study found that peer-to-peer recognition was nearly 36 percent more likely to have a positive impact on financial results than manager-only recognition.[2] When employees receive recognition or feedback exclusively from their manager, there is only one definitive voice being heard. But when we invite others into the conversation and everyone feels invested in a culture of feedback, we hear a chorus of voices.

DIVERSITY REDUCES BIAS. Seeking more voices promotes inclusion and brings us broad and diverse perspectives. Increasing the points of view lessens the impact of unconscious bias from any single individual.

ONE BITE IS RIGHT

Clearly, I want you to seek focused feedback frequently. What I don't want you to do is bite off more than you can chew. Be sure that the skill, topic, or behavior you choose to focus your seeking and improvement efforts on is meaningful enough to make a difference, yet narrow enough to be something you can make progress on within a reasonable time frame. Moreover, stay focused on one thing at a time. Trying to work on multiple agendas will only dilute your success and increase your frustration. It's like taking golf lessons from an overeager coach who's doling out a steady stream of swing thoughts for you to try to manage: *Keep your head down, don't overswing, turn your shoulders and hips together* . . . Enough! One thing at a time, please! Trust me, maintaining a narrow focus will keep you in your happy place, make it easy for those around you to help, and prevent you from hurling your mental club into the feedback pond in anger.

ASK FOR THE GOOD STUFF

Don't shy away from the good stuff. I encourage you to shore up your strengths, hone the crafts you love and excel at, and find your superpowers. Playing to your strengths is the secret to a happy and meaningful life. So, if they're that important, we better know what they are and how, when we let our strengths shine, they bring value to others. And the best way to know is simply to ask.

As you strive to recognize your strengths, take along these two pearls of wisdom borrowed from Marcus Buckingham, the "Strengths Guru":

• Your strengths are not what you're good at, and your weaknesses are not what you're bad at. If you're good at something, but it drains you—that's not a strength, that's a weakness. A strength is an activity that makes you *feel* strong, just as a weakness is an activity that makes you feel weak.

- You will grow the most, learn the most, and develop the most in your areas of strength. Your strengths are your areas of opportunity for growth, so when looking to invest, put your effort there!

Make sure your seeking strategy helps you recognize the things you love, then let that insight help you fall in love with your work. There is no better gift to yourself or your organization.

> I've seen a lot of compelling speakers in my years, but one presentation that has stuck with me was delivered by a photographer from *National Geographic*. Using stunning photos to illustrate his points, he juxtaposed what we witness in nature with lessons we can learn in life. In one illustrative example, he shared his experience of watching seagulls flying off the cliffs of Hawaii. Many of the birds were soaring on the wind, and he noted that in watching them soar he could see their grace and ease, as well as the joy of just letting the winds carry them. Then he turned his attention to those birds who were flying into the wind, flapping their hearts out while making slow progress against nature. He went on to point out that in life there are times when we soar and times when we flap. It wasn't hard to recognize that same phenomenon in my own life. I thought about days or projects that felt like soaring, and I could recall the joy they brought. My thoughts also turned to the struggles I'd had, and I felt for those birds who were flapping as hard as they could just to stay aloft. I'll bet it's not hard for you to summon memories of soaring and flapping yourself. Wouldn't we all be better off and a little happier if we found ways to do more soaring and less flapping?
>
> *Tamra*

FIND YOUR
BLIND SPOTS

One of the very first lessons we get in driver's ed is to watch out for blind spots, the sections on either side of the road behind us that aren't visible in our side-view mirrors and where danger may lurk. We all have personal or work-related blind spots, too. During the process of becoming a Seeker, we need to be mindful of what may be hidden from view in these areas.

Sleuthing out your blind spots is not a journey for the timid, but it can lead to profound outcomes. On the next page you'll find a great exercise we use at PeopleFirm to reveal blind spots. You'll want to be especially deliberate about who you choose to help you with this exercise; turn to a trusted friend or advisor.

EXERCISE: BUILDING MUSCLE AROUND BLIND SPOTS

1. For a week, use the Fine Art of Noticing to ask for blind-spot feedback from one person each day. It might be as simple as this:

   "Is there anything about me that I don't seem to see when I'm interacting with my customers, but is obvious to you?"

2. Never ask the same person twice.

3. Listen to and compare the feedback you get. Any "aha's" there? Then make your plan to grow and improve.

During the early stages of writing this book, I was sharing the topic of feedback with an elderly friend of my mother's, who explained that one of her bold and outspoken grandchildren recently told her that she was known as the family complainer. (Mind you, she described this exchange as friendly, not contentious.) Her grandchild had said, "Gramma, everyone knows that all you do is talk about your medical stuff, and that is why no one wants to visit with you very much." The 80-year-old said she was totally blind to this and just thought that the lack of connection with her grandkids came down to generational differences. She lamented, "Imagine if someone had the kindness to tell me that 20 years ago. I might have done something about it and maybe I could have had very different relationships with my grandkids now."

Seekers, I implore you not to wait until it's too late to become this wise. Wonder what immense possibilities are out there for you if you simply seek insights into your blind spots? Not sure what kind of feedback to seek? Sounds like a good time to start asking others!

Laura

FOCUS ON PROGRESS

Messed something up recently? Fell short of your target? Missed a key performance metric? Then by all means cop to it as you seek, but don't make your *mea culpa* the focus of the conversation. Quickly move on to ask for coaching that can help you succeed the next time around.

If you say, "I missed this target and I feel badly about it. Now I'm looking for some guidance on specifically how to clean this up and avoid another miss next month. Would you be willing to help me think this through?" it's more likely to get you to where you need to go than, "Oh, man, I missed my target. I'm hopeless!"

Focusing on what you need (not necessarily on what you want) and when you need it to achieve the specific progress you're targeting makes it more likely that you'll take in and retain the feedback, then use it in a way that is effective for you.

FOCUS ON THE FUTURE

At this point I feel compelled to remind you what all this asking is about. It's about your future. It's about your aspirations. As you set out on your seeking journey, don't lose sight of the ultimate goal: building a better you.

In this rapidly changing and complex world, we also need to allow for flexibility and give ourselves some grace when our expectations change, when we're in the midst of learning something new about ourselves, or as the demands of work evolve. Whether your dreams hold strong or bend with the wind, you as Seeker are in charge. You can choose to stay the course or opt for a detour based on what you're learning. Regardless of your path or your career status, keep your development agenda and objectives front and center and let feedback fuel your targeted growth and learning.

MAKE A PLAN

Want to be sure your seeking is successful? Make a plan! Here are a few reminders to help you get going:

- Begin with the end in mind and work backward. Keep your eyes on the prize—your future—and let that guide what you're seeking.
- Make a list of the people who can help. Remember to diversify your ask by engaging people who bring different perspectives. Validate your list with others to help you discover people you might be missing.
- Prepare to ask for focused feedback on a topic important to you. Consider what one question, if answered, would bring the most value.
- Connect first. Start small and take it one step at a time.
- Ask in advance and share your Feedback Guide with those you've asked.
- Give your Extenders some time to do some "noticing."

Above all, pause often to celebrate your progress and openly share your gratitude with those who've contributed to the better you. Oh, and offer to do the same for them. After all, the feedback revolution will be built one connection at a time.

RECEIVERS

RECIPIENTS OF FEEDBACK, SOUGHT OR UNSOUGHT, WANTED OR UNWANTED

CHAPTER 7

RECEIVING FEEDBACK

WHEN YOU'RE A RECEIVER, someone is offering you information they think you need or want. Affirming or challenging, solicited or unsolicited, relevant or irrelevant, your goal is to take the feedback in, and, ideally, resist knee-jerk reactions in favor of making thoughtful choices about how you'll respond.

When you find yourself in the receiving role, your goal is to bring your best self to the situation, so there's no room for lashing out, clamming up, or fleeing the scene altogether. If what you're hearing is making your heart race and your hands shake, you know it's time to put fear in its place. Breathe, feel your feet, and let your wise brain catch up and take charge. You don't have to accept all the feedback that is handed to you, but listening to it with an open mind is a great first step.

LEADERS GO FIRST

Leaders have a responsibility to demonstrate how to receive feedback with integrity and grace. Why? Because all eyes will be on you. You set the tone: you've started a movement, and now you've got to model how it's done. To help ready your receiving self, tune into these proven leader practices:

BE THE CHANGE YOU WANT TO SEE. There's no quicker way to shut down our movement than failing to step up and listen to what others have to offer. You need to make the commitment to do the same work you'll be asking of your people.

RECOGNIZE THAT RECEIVING MAKES YOU STRONGER. If you think asking for and gathering feedback makes you look like a weaker leader, think again. Folkman and Zenger's research links a leader's preferences for asking for and sharing positive feedback to an uptick in nearly every measure of leadership competency.

MAKE IT SAFE. People are far more likely to tell you the truth when they feel safe. You have positional power as a leader, so assure your people that they can share what they've noticed without suffering repercussions.

RECEIVE WITH GRACE. You may not love everything you hear. Nonetheless, your mission is to receive feedback with grace and appreciation. In short: listen, clarify, express gratitude, and follow up.

BE FEARLESSLY AUTHENTIC. Everyone knows you're only human, so they won't be surprised if you show up that way. It's okay to be authentic and vulnerable; in fact, people crave those behaviors from their leaders. Identify the areas in which you're willing to share more, then let down those barriers. I can tell you from experience that trust gets a shot in the arm when you share your imperfections.

KNOW YOUR FEEDBACK SELF

Our emotional responses to feedback have much to do with our self-image and core beliefs. Depending on the nature of the feedback, this can either work for us or against us. For example, if a colleague tells you that your creative thinking brings consistent value to your organization, that's likely to bring a smile to your face. It will also reinforce your belief that creativity is one of your core capabilities. However, if you feel that tenacity is one of your strong points, then having your manager say that you gave up too easily on a sale is likely to shake that belief. When feedback really strikes a nerve, it may be because it's veering dangerously close to the core of your very being.

As Receivers, it's helpful to take stock of what we value and believe about ourselves. Increasing our awareness of what we hold dear helps us modulate and understand our feedback responses when someone scores a direct hit and sinks one of our emotional battleships. Knowledge is power, and the more we understand ourselves, the more open we can be with others.

Years ago, I was a market leader at a large consulting firm, working a project with our head of HR. One morning over coffee he told me that he'd noticed that most of my work was driven by collaboration. He went on to say that he believed my collaborative style would limit my career. (I have to confess that telling you this story raises my blood pressure, even after all these years.) Despite my anger, I still managed to give his feedback some honest reflection, and I tested his perspective with some trusted colleagues. In the end, I made the choice to say, "Thanks, but no thanks. I'm sticking to my guns." Taking the time for serious reflection enabled me to confirm that collaboration was one of my unshakable values, and it's subsequently proven to be key to any success I've achieved in my career.

HITTING RESET

As we gathered feedback stories for this book, it was eye-opening to hear the stories that involved Receivers reacting poorly to what Extenders were sharing with them. In many of these stories, the Receivers eventually found their way toward accepting the feedback, and that acceptance ended up changing their outlooks, their jobs, or even their lives. Now that you've joined the movement, you may need to bring those alienated Extenders back in the feedback arena with you. Here's how:

APOLOGIZE. Relationship repair is tricky. How bad was it? If you yelled or threw things, then you have some work to do. Honestly share what it was that triggered your response. You could say something like "Hey, I'm sorry about getting angry when you were reviewing my team's performance data yesterday. The thing is, we're proud of what we've accomplished, so it's frustrating to feel like we're being judged strictly by the numbers. Now that I've had time to reflect, can we discuss this further sometime soon?"

DON'T OVER-APOLOGIZE. On the flip side, don't go overboard. One brief and authentic apology is all that's needed. No one wants to repeatedly assure you that it's okay when they'd much prefer to reset and move on.

LOOP BACK AROUND. Has anyone ever offered you feedback that you initially resisted but later came to accept as valuable? Even if it was years ago, I implore you to let that person know how that feedback ended up impacting your work or your life.

SAVOR THE GOOD STUFF

When you receive a tasty morsel of positive feedback, do you feel yourself actively listening, or do you default to minimizing the impact of your contribution or deflecting all the credit to others? There's a lot to be gained by allowing yourself to celebrate. Here's how to stop the deflection and use this newfound knowledge to move you forward:

SAY, "THANK YOU." PERIOD. Curb that inner critic who tries to deflect and decline.

INQUIRE IF APPROPRIATE. If it's appropriate (for example, a rapid round of gratitude-sharing during a team meeting might not be the right time), ask questions about specifics and look for trends. You could approach a colleague or mentor with "Thanks for the great noticing. Can I ask exactly what you found helpful about my research on the roadmap?"

SHARE THE CREDIT. Had a partner? A helping hand? Part of a successful team project? Find ways to share the credit without minimizing your role.

AVOID DEFLECTING OR ASKING FOR ADDITIONAL RE-ASSURANCE. Try to receive recognition with unassuming gratitude. Saying, "Really? I felt like I completely botched the speech," or "Oh, it was not that big a deal," might seem like humility, but those comments can devalue the feedback and make the person who gave you the compliment feel as though you question their judgment.

REFLECT AND GROW. Reflect on the things you're consistently told you're good at. Understand what's driving the appreciation, and what it might mean for your plan and your future. Find ways to hone these strengths to create an even better and more impactful you.

KICK SOME ASK

Kicking some serious ask isn't just for when you're in Seeker mode; it can also be helpful to gain clarity and more actionable learnings when receiving feedback. This is especially true if your Extender is struggling to provide you specifics or fact-based insights.

Let's look at a few common scenarios and some sample phrases you might employ to help you get the most out of every receiving opportunity:

When you're not getting helpful specifics:

CLARIFY THE CONTEXT. "Can you share with me when or where you noticed this?"

ASK FOR THE SPECIFICS. "Can you give me more details? What exactly did you notice?"

ASK ABOUT THE EFFECT. "Can you say more about the impact I had on you or others?"

When it's just a little too much:

ONE THING. "What is the one thing you think I should do more or less of?"

REQUEST FOCUS. "If you were to focus your perspective into a single idea, what would the headline be?"

When they're struggling to get to the point:

MAKE IT SAFE. "It seems like you're trying to tell me something important. I'm really interested in what it is."

ASK FOR WHAT YOU NEED. "What I'm really working on is _____. Are you seeing me make progress toward that goal?"

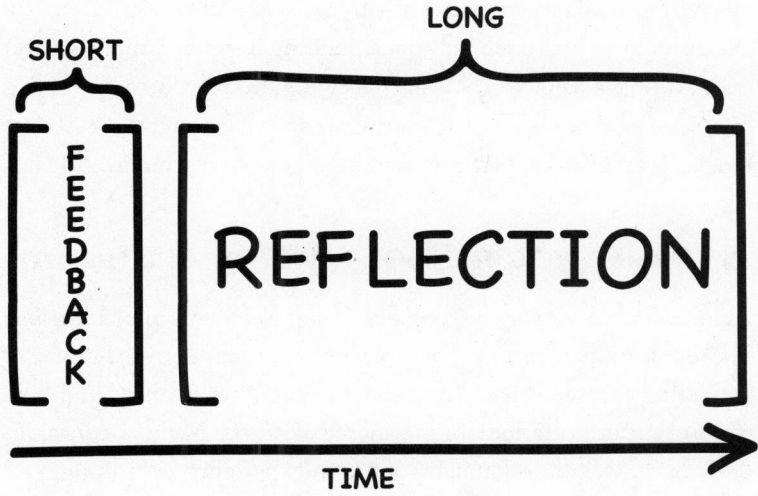

FEEDBACK SHORT, REFLECTION LONG

I have a little idea that could offer big results. There will be times when an Extender hands you a bite-size bit of feedback that eventually leads to something huge. Remember my story about a colleague at Hitachi who remarked that she hadn't seen me so engaged in a topic in years? After she casually served up that bit of noticing, I thought about it for months. I rolled it around in my mind and looked at it from all angles. I considered whether or not it was true, and if it was true, why? I tested it and validated it with others. I considered the implications. I connected it with other trends in my behavior. While the feedback was short, my reflection was long and, in the end, life-changing. It was the gentle breath of wind that began a monumental journey that's included the founding of PeopleFirm, the writing of this book, and so much more.

This is the craziness and the beauty of our new definition of feedback. It's the little things that, when we're tuned in to seeking, extending, and receiving them, can change everything. They can close old doors and open new ones, sending us off on unfamiliar yet exhilarating adventures. When receiving, you need to savor this bite-size feedback and let it marinate in your consciousness for as long as it takes to extract every grain of goodness from it.

I'M ~~RIGHT,~~ YOU'RE ~~RIGHT,~~ WE'RE ALL HUMAN

Remember that array of cognitive biases we discussed earlier? Those biases are not only the gremlins that can get in the way of extending fair feedback. They also impact what we hear and how we process information that is shared with us. Make a conscious decision to weigh how much your own experiences, thinking, and beliefs might be influencing your interpretation of the conversation. If you don't, then negativity bias may sidetrack your wise brain.

One distortion that can occur when we're receiving feedback, especially from a less accomplished Extender, is to conflate their intent with the impact we feel. If you conclude that your manager called out that typo on your slide deck because she wanted to embarrass you in front of her boss, you're making an assumption about her intent that may well be false.

To avoid this common trap, our best strategy as Receivers is to assume positive intent. Ignore that little voice in your head that's saying, "Danger!" Instead, tell yourself that the person speaking has no hidden agenda and only the best intentions. Reinforce your own thinking that this feedback has been extended to benefit you, not harm you.

When you first start assuming positive intent, you may feel vulnerable. After all, you're asking yourself to be open to a new way of thinking. Further, you may have very good reason to question an individual's motives, especially if you've had a bad experience with them in the past. Sometimes you can ease that feeling of vulnerability by simply asking about their intent. A direct question like "What are you hoping to accomplish with this discussion?" may lead to a candid and illuminating exchange.

Remember that we're all works in process, so please don't shoot (i.e., ignore) the messenger based on bad delivery. As you turn up your seeking volume, you're bound to be exposed to a wider array of Extender styles and competence. It's unavoidable that some of that feedback will continue to be delivered in that same old clunky manner. Patience is crucial. Not everyone will be part of our movement, nor will we all immediately hone the skills of an accomplished Extender. And unskilled doesn't mean unworthy. So if you find yourself in the Receiver seat wanting to clobber your Extender with a copy of this book, forgo the thumping, give them a little grace, and use your new feedback chops to increase the benefits of the exchange for both of you.

YOU'RE NOT LOVING WHAT YOU'RE HEARING?

Wouldn't it be great if all feedback met every one of the lofty standards that make up our new definition of the word? Clearly, it doesn't; if it did, our feedback-fixing movement would have no reason to exist.

Feedback that's nonspecific, vague, not future-focused or growth-oriented, or just plain mean-spirited can send you into a spiral of confusion, shame, or resentment. Conversely, tough but effective feedback might get your pulse racing at first, yet once you've got yourself into a more receptive mindset and you recognize the value of what's been offered, you may experience that combination of exhaustion and exhilaration that follows a good workout.

Either way, by practicing good receiving techniques, you'll be able to get an accurate picture of what's being communicated to you, giving you the ability to make an informed decision about what to do with the feedback you're not "feeling." You may choose to dismiss it altogether or swallow hard and accept whatever truths you can glean. Here are a few helpful pointers on gracefully handling feedback you're not loving:

DON'T RUSH TO REACT. Start with a simple "thank you" and give yourself time to process. Your initial reaction may be very different from the one you'll have after hearing more and reflecting on what's being said. Everyone benefits when you absorb the feedback without defensiveness or deflection.

SWITCH FROM PROVE TO IMPROVE. If you're finding yourself defending your position and wanting to prove the Receiver wrong, try switching your mindset from "prove" mode to "improve" mode. Doing so will allow you to hear insights that could help you down the road.

INQUIRE FOR FACTS AND EXAMPLES. If what you got was a bit vague ("Just watch what Candice does and follow suit"), then mine for facts that may lie beneath the surface. Create clarity by asking questions that can help the Extender get more specific: "What exactly did Candice do that you would like me to focus on next time?" or "What is the most important thing you would have me pay attention to?"

BUST BIAS AND ASSUMPTIONS TOGETHER. Does it feel like facts have taken a holiday? Is the Extender basing feedback on an assumption or an illusion about you? If you suspect this may be the case, have the courage to ask the Extender to help you test their assumptions with some open questions:

- "Are you willing to test that assumption with me? Can we walk through your thinking together?"
- "I feel like that could be an assumption being made about me. Would you share the facts or observations that led to this conclusion?"

ASK FOR A PAUSE IF YOU NEED IT. A simple "Hey, I'm listening, but I'd like to process this before we talk further" will do. Reschedule if you feel agitated or unprepared to ask for clarification without coming across as defensive (4-7-8 breathing helps here).

SEEK ADDITIONAL SOURCES OF CLARITY. Still unsure? Go back to seeking. If you feel there is a nugget of information worth mining there, but you still don't have enough to process or plan around, call on your Extender network to do some noticing for you.

SEEK SUPPORT, BUT NOT TRIANGULATION. Research has shown that social support reduces stress. However, don't use this as an opportunity to vent or triangulate. Texting, "Drinks, STAT!" to a friend after every feedback encounter is not likely to be a great processing aid. In fact, if you're really stirred up about the feedback, this venting (also known as "wine and whine") usually doesn't help, and it can actually add more stress to your situation. Instead, ask a mentor or peer to help you think through what you've heard. Give them the full picture in advance so they come prepared to engage, and present your questions in an open manner, without your own judgment attached.

IT'S FINE TO DECLINE. If it's unhelpful or even hurtful feedback (perhaps it's coming from someone who's not in a good head space, or who simply doesn't have your best interests in mind), then the best strategy may be to say, "Thanks, but no thanks." Focus your energy on the information your gut tells you is valuable.

PROGRESS, NOT PUNISHMENT

We've all done it, and most of us will do it again. I'm talking about overreacting, magnifying or distorting what we heard, or harboring bad feelings. One slice of feedback and *bam!* We're in a downward spiral.

This is a common human response. Psychologist Susan Nolen-Hoeksema has demonstrated that our memories and thoughts are threaded together in the brain and not compartmentalized. When any single stressor is activated, the ensuing bad feelings can unlock a flood of other negative thoughts that are unrelated to the initial trigger.[1]

The best thing we can do once we've launched ourselves into one of these downward spirals is to show ourselves a little (or maybe a lot of) compassion, regain control, and then shift our focus to progress instead of punishment. When you find yourself in this situation, move past the self-incrimination by reflecting on these simple questions:

- What's scary about what I heard? How bad was it, really?
- What's the one thing I least want to accept?
- What do I sense is true about this?
- What do I reject as false or biased?
- How might it impact my future direction?
- Where do I go from here? What would progress look like?

These ideas may be helpful as well:

FIND A TRUSTED FRIEND. Ask a confidant or mentor to help you work through it. An outside perspective can be crucial to escaping your negative thought patterns.

DON'T GET STUCK. Don't let this feedback define you and get you stuck in a fixed mindset about who you are and what you can and can't do. Instead, define what actions or outcomes would demonstrate incremental progress and start your journey.

FOLLOW UP. Once you've determined your next steps, check in on your progress. Ask for more noticing in the future.

STAY THE COURSE. The path of progress is never a straight line, so stay the course and be kind to yourself along the way. Know that you'll learn as much from your setbacks as you do from your successes.

GIVE YOURSELF SOME GRACE. When we set out to change a pattern or overcome a fear, we're striving for a new level of mastery. It doesn't happen overnight, so give yourself some space to make and measure progress without obsessing about the ultimate result.

FOCUS ON THE FUTURE

Feedback is about guiding the path to your future self, so consider positive feedback and recommendations on areas of growth and improvement in the context of your future goals:

- Will this information propel me closer to my goals?
- Does it challenge my view of my future self? (Maybe you've got superpowers you hadn't previously considered.)
- Does it change my options or my plan? Does it open new doors?
- Does it add clarity about the work I need to do?
- What is it telling me about what I should do more or less of?

MAKE A PLAN

For Receivers, your plan here is less about your feedback strategy than it is about your growth and development plan. Once you've processed the feedback you've received, make your choices about what you'll do with it and how you'll track your progress. Here are a few planning tips to get you started:

MAKE YOUR LIST, THEN CHOOSE. As you receive feedback, keep track of what you're hearing. As you move to the planning stage, look for trends, test it against your future aspirations, and then pick the one thing you'll start with. Remember, don't boil the ocean. One bite is right!

COCREATE. Sometimes it's helpful to sit with a trusted advisor (maybe your boss or a colleague who knows you well) and create your plan together. Two brains are almost always better than one.

TRACK PROGRESS WITH MORE SEEKING. As you set your course for growth and development, check in with others to see if they are noticing the work you're doing. Take note of suggested course corrections and celebrate the advances you are logging.

EXTENDERS

INDIVIDUALS WHO GIVE FEEDBACK TO OTHERS, EITHER PROACTIVELY OR BY REQUEST

CHAPTER 8

EXTENDING FEEDBACK

THINKING THIS ROLE ISN'T about you? Think again! Sure, in the feedback world we're hoping to leave behind, the Extender role has typically fallen to a manager or team leader. But as you and your colleagues accept the challenge to seek first and seek often in our new feedback frontier, all of us should get comfortable in the hot seat of extending. If you *are* a manager or team leader, won't it be nice to have everyone else practicing the art of noticing right along with you?

As an Extender, your mission is to engage with anyone and everyone, whether they work with you, for you, or above you. You need to be available when asked and willing to offer when the time is right. Your feedback should be authentic, specific, focused, and free of judgment. That's a lot of responsibility, but you can tackle this role with confidence and courage once you're armed with the knowledge and skills needed for successful extending.

CREATE CONNECTIONS

Remember the 5:1 ratio? It tells us that positive connections build trust. The more the merrier, since connections build relationships, and trusted relationships are the Holy Grail of Feedback. As our relationships strengthen, our positive influence on one another intensifies. The quality, relevance, and focus of our feedback is likely to improve. What's more, our feedback is much more likely to fall on fully engaged and receptive ears.

If all this connecting business sounds like a lot of work, take comfort in the fact that, according to research, connecting is really not that hard. After all, we as humans crave positive connections. This is not scary stuff, it's feel-good stuff. So what's the key to making connecting a habit? Frequency. I'm betting you will need to increase the frequency with which you connect with those around you.

To help you get going, here are a few ideas for revving up your connection motor:

TAKE NOTICE, TAKE INTEREST. Be inquisitive and display sincere interest in what's going on around you. Ask open-ended questions, acknowledge workloads, and praise daily progress.

LET GO OF POSITIONAL POWER. Let others talk first. If you are a leader, don't automatically take your traditional seat at meetings; mix it up by allowing someone else to sit there, especially if it's at the head of the table. Ask others, "What's the most important thing you'd like to talk about today?" instead of habitually pushing your agenda. The conversation that ensues could be the best takeaway from the meeting, and your people will know that their input has real value to you.

GRATITUDE AND APPRECIATION. Every time you express positive thoughts, appreciation, or gratitude, you strengthen relationships and build trust. Just make sure it's real, because cheap is cheap, and people can spot a fake a mile away.

FIND A COMMON POINT OF VIEW. When we seek ways to agree with another's viewpoint, we validate that they matter to us, and that they can trust us to have their best interests in mind.

PURPOSEFUL COLLABORATION. Take on a tough challenge with a person you have a sticky relationship with and see if you can't open avenues for trust. When we try to understand another point of view, collaborate with and challenge one another, we begin to understand one another's strengths, patterns, and emotional triggers. Knowledge of others is a critical component to building trust.

HELP OTHERS. Life is full of opportunities to "carry water" for others. Maybe we help assemble that final report, give a coworker a ride home, or grab some takeout for the assistant who's too slammed to get lunch.

EMPATHIZE. Empathy is one of the deepest forms of human connection. When you empathize with another, you show that you are trying to understand and feel what they feel. Saying things like "I understand why you're feeling overwhelmed about making this deadline" tells them that they are connected and that you're concerned not only with their performance but also with their emotional well-being.

LIGHTEN UP. Make time to have a little fun. Sharing a good laugh over a cup of coffee can dramatically lower stress, increase connections, and build trust.

LEADERS GO FIRST

For a lot of leaders, seeking and receiving feedback is about learning new skills and building new muscles. However, when it comes to extending, it's more about fine-tuning an already established approach.

As leaders, we'll need to let go of old habits and traditional practices and embrace a new model, one that's anchored in our three fabulous Fs:

- Fairness in your approach, free of assumptions and punishment
- Focused coaching for targeted growth
- Frequent, positive connections, light and easy

As a leader, you're showing the way, setting the tone, and walking the talk of our feedback movement. Sure, this new regimen is good for your people, but there's plenty in it for you, too. Frequent sharing is helping you build more optimal responses to giving and getting feedback, and it's also making you a better leader.

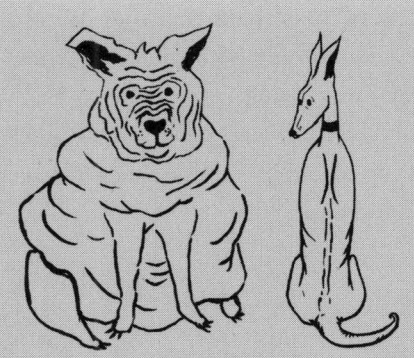

We're no longer body-building for bulk with infrequent, heavy-handed feedback discussions; instead, we're shifting to developing long and lean feedback muscles for speed and agility, focusing on light, informal, frequent touchpoints.

SHARE THE LOAD: BE A FEEDBACK MULTIPLIER

As I deliver workshops around the world, the dread of a thousand weary managers hangs heavy in the room when I ask even more of them: *more* connections, *more* feedback, *more* frequency. They're asking themselves, "How can I possibly do more when I'm barely able to keep up with the coaching, mentoring, and reviewing I'm already doing?" Here's the thing: I'm not suggesting managers do it all, but I am asking them to lead the movement and show the way. As leaders, it's up to them to demonstrate the benefits of seeking more sources of feedback and upping its frequency while encouraging their people to do the same. In this way, leaders will become *feedback multipliers*. Leaders who proactively recruit those around them to become part of the frequent feedback movement will reap the rewards of the growth they inspire in their own backyards.

KNOW YOUR FEEDBACK SELF

It takes two to tango. That old saying has relevance here. In every feedback encounter, the tone and the quality of the experience is highly dependent on how *all* of the players show up. As one of the partners in the feedback tango, Extenders need to mind their steps, taking accountability for their approach to every conversation and for their true intentions. To be sure you're well prepared when the dance begins, take the time to reflect on these three questions:

1. **DO YOU UNDERSTAND THE INFLUENCE YOUR OWN STYLE, PERSPECTIVES, AND PERSONALITY HAVE ON YOUR APPROACH?**
   » What seems open and direct to one person can seem harsh and sharp to another. You may get a little juice from a public call-out of your contributions, but your peer finds it horribly uncomfortable. Everyone is unique, so proceed with caution and never assume your Receivers want feedback delivered in the same manner or tone as you do. Answering this question honestly requires some careful self-reflection about how your style and personality influence your thinking and manner. For each of us, there will be times we need to adjust our approach or tone to better suit the individual we're trying to recognize or help.

2. **ARE YOU CLEAR ON YOUR INTENTIONS?**
   » Sometimes we rush to extend feedback before we've really taken the time to check in on why we feel compelled to do so. All of us can fall victim at times to less-than-perfect intentions. Maybe we're feeling a little bruised from a project that didn't go well, and we're wanting to share a bit of the blame; maybe we're trying to make a point that we don't think is being heard. We've all been there, so it's always good to pause long enough to consider a few of these questions:
   o What am I feeling right now that is prompting me to consider extending this feedback?

- o   Is this the real issue?
- o   Is this really just about me and not about the other person?

3. **ARE YOU ENTERING THE CONVERSATION WITH A FIXED MINDSET OR A GROWTH MINDSET?**

   » As discussed earlier, we can have a fixed mindset about ourselves and about others. Knowing this, check in with yourself before you engage. Are you coming to the table with a true belief that improvement or growth is possible? Is the intent of your feedback aimed at that growth?

Highly resilient people are much admired in business settings. In fact, they are often placed in leadership roles. Their ability to respond to difficult situations without losing their cool usually serves them and those they lead well. Also, highly resilient people are often quite proud of their ability to keep calm and remain focused and analytical when times get tough. This capacity is almost universally regarded as a strength.

There can be a downside to this strength in the realm of feedback, however, so here's a word of warning to the highly resilient feedback provider, whether you are in a leadership role or not. Sometimes your cool and calm outlook can blind you to how powerful your words can be when you extend feedback. Imagine the cool, resilient person providing a more sensitive one some difficult messaging in a highly matter-of-fact manner. Sometimes that can be good, but if the Receiver is overwhelmed by the messaging, or just not in a good emotional place to absorb it, the resilient person's demeanor can come off as rough and cold. This can cause the Receiver to feel a level of impact that is utterly unintended, and it has the potential to cause long-term damage to a trusted relationship. So for you highly resilient types, it will serve you well to cultivate awareness of how your words and demeanor are impacting the Receivers of your messaging. Before you jump in, ask if the time is right to talk, indicating the subject you're wanting to discuss. Be clear that you come in peace and start from a place of trust.

Laura

HITTING RESET: APOLOGIZE IF NEEDED

If you've dug deeply enough into your feedback past, you've probably unearthed more than a few cringe-worthy moments when you've failed as an Extender. News flash: that's true for everyone. We're human. It's okay. And when it comes to reconnecting with Receivers who were left shaking their heads by those encounters, a little humility goes a long way.

Acknowledge and apologize. Hit the reset button on prickly relationships by swallowing your pride and asking for a redo on that conversation you handled clumsily. Sure, it may feel awkward, but a sincere apology can begin the process of reestablishing trust and fairness. Admit that you're a work in progress and assure them that you're sincerely seeking to improve and that you believe things can indeed be different. An apology might sound something like this: "I'm sorry I was in command-and-control mode the last time we spoke. I'm trying to get better at feedback and would really appreciate it if you'd give me a do-over. Could you and I talk about our project plan today and give this another shot?"

You can't take back what you've said or done in the past, but you can address it honestly and humbly and then commit to getting better. I'm betting you'll be surprised by how much goodwill will result from a simple and authentic apology.

KICK SOME ASK

Asking is not just for Seekers. When playing the role of Extender, you can set the stage for successful feedback by asking the right questions. Here are a few asks to consider:

ASK FIRST. Offering unsolicited feedback is a high-risk proposition. You might leave the Receiver feeling blindsided, and, intentionally or not, it places you in a position of power over the Receiver. Here are several ways to look before you leap:

- Be gracious. Ask for permission to share.
- Ask if this is a good time or if another time would be better.

- Ask if this is a good place to talk. If it's not, find an appropriate space, maybe something more private or comfortable where you and the Receiver feel safe and are able to speak freely.

ASK HOW. One way to bring more fairness to your feedback is by simply asking people when and how they want to receive feedback. In the Receiver chapter I gave you a feedback guide to complete. When you're in the Extender role, ask those you're working with to share their guide with you. This will help you learn the nature of the feedback they'll value most, what tends to push their buttons, and how to get the best from them. Teams and peers who are encouraged to extend feedback often find it helpful to be armed with some boundaries and guidelines for how to connect with one another. It typically takes no more than 10 minutes to validate how an individual wants to receive feedback, and it sets your relationship up for success. Give it a try!

COME WITH QUESTIONS, NOT ANSWERS. When we fully embrace the Fine Art of Noticing, we have observations to share that are extended without judgment or evaluation. Whether we're sharing because we were asked by a Seeker, or our offer to share was accepted by a Receiver, we can enhance the quality of the conversation with well-placed questions. Powerful and focused questions help the Receiver move toward progress and away from a defensive stature. They help us, as the Extender, check our assumptions and learn how we can be of more value to the Receiver.

I received some feedback myself about my feedback fairness just last year from Raine, one of our senior consultants. I thought I was being so "in the moment" with my feedback. Real-time feedback is what we are aiming for, right? I texted Raine, who was at that very moment hosting a live webinar attended by hundreds of our clients and potential clients on a topic on which she is very knowledgeable. The mics were live and I was listening in across town. Raine was sounding scripted to me, a little bit tense, a little too animated. I dashed off a quick text that said, "Lighten up, tone it down a little bit. You're doing fine." I was coaching, connecting, encouraging, and doing so in the moment, right? That's the way I'd like it and I'm sure she'll find it helpful, I thought. Wrong! Raine later told me that my text, received without invitation and during the live webinar, was one of the most unfair pieces of feedback she had ever received. "What the hell was I supposed to do with that feedback right in that very moment?" she asked, then added, "I began to doubt every word coming out of my mouth, and we still had 30 minutes of the webinar to get through." While my intention was good, that feedback was not asked for, and in hindsight my timing was unfair. Raine let me know that the text certainly did not help her to "switch it up" in the moment; instead it made her self-conscious and left her wondering if she was annoying everyone else on the call as well, if we were going to publish the thing on social media or pull it from our channels, and all kinds of other unhelpful thoughts that no doubt distracted her from the task at hand. I'm grateful she spoke to me later and was honest about how my attempt at feedback had impacted her. We had a conversation about how and when she would like to receive feedback from me in the future, and I learned that it certainly wasn't "live when the mics are on." I learned a lot from Raine that day. I thought that "in the moment" meant anytime and any place. I prefer my feedback that way, so I mistakenly assumed she would feel the same. I learned the hard way that one size and style does not fit all! Respecting the diversity of ways that people think and feel about feedback increases the fairness.

Laura

SHARE THE GOOD STUFF

Now that you've given some thought to the concept of the Gottman 5:1 connection ratio and the Fine Art of Noticing, I'm betting you've tuned into the idea that positive, fact-based noticing, combined with genuine and positive connections, should happen at a rate that's five times greater than challenging or correcting feedback.

When sharing the good stuff, be heartfelt and effusive. However, facts and details are important here. People only trust praise when it's anchored in descriptive fact and offered without judgment or labels. No one's going to object to hearing, "You're the best!" But let's be real: it's a subjective judgment, a label, it's not very clear, and it doesn't help anyone understand how (or why) to continue to be "the best."

When sharing the good stuff, consider these tips:

DESCRIBE THE GOOD. Instead of general praise, how much more skillful and effective would it be if descriptive facts were added? It might look like this: "Great job on the Wilson account, Yoshi. I noticed it came in under budget and on time, and you were responsible for three new client testimonials on our website."

MANAGERS AND TEAM LEADERS SET THE PACE. Nearly every manager overestimates the volume and influence of their positive feedback. Research tells us that managers are rarely as effusive and impactful when it comes to sharing the good as they self-assess.[1] As noted in chapter 2, leaders are also likely to overestimate the importance that sharing improvement feedback has to their people and their leadership brand. In the end, we know the real power for leaders is in sharing positive feedback. Upping the volume and frequency on recognition of progress, successes, strong performance—in short, contributions both large and small—is a leader's best strategy for influencing the performance of their team and raising their own leadership brand in the eyes of those who work for them.

BUILD GREAT TEAM HABITS. Establish team and peer feedback opportunities and encourage everyone to seek and extend feedback that moves the team forward. Make sure you recognize teams and groups, and that you share appropriate kudos publicly while not forgetting that some people prefer private recognition. I'm a big fan of building team habits for recognition and feedback as it builds our collective feedback muscles and begins to anchor this behavior as a group norm.

FOCUS YOUR INTENT AND AVOID THE SH*T SANDWICH

> **sh*t sandwich** *(plural* sh*t sandwiches)
> **1.** /SHit/ /ˈsan‚(d)wiCH/ (*informal, vulgar*) Something highly undesirable made triflingly more palatable by attempting to surround it with more tolerable things.

Most of us have been exposed to the feedback staple we call—ahem—the sh*t sandwich. In fact, the concept is so prevalent that it's defined in Wikipedia.

People tend to avoid giving others "critical feedback." It's uncomfortable. It stirs up our fears of being disliked, disregarded, or disowned. So, when faced with the challenge of sharing something we fear might be tough to swallow, we think it may go down a little easier if we sandwich our tough feedback between two soft, tasty slices of compliment.

If you're slapping a sh*t sandwich together, especially if you're known to do it repeatedly, the Receiver will have no problem sniffing it out. Everything you're sharing becomes suspect. You've created distrust and you've unintentionally tainted future interactions.

When we receive a *genuine* compliment or offer of gratitude, connection happens. It's straightforward and unambiguously honest. Trust increases and fear decreases. The problem with the sh*t sandwich is that the good stuff on the outside is fouled by the nastiness in the middle, even when it's genuine.

So how do we avoid the urge to slap together this mess?

- Focus. When you need to focus on a tough conversation, just do it. Do it skillfully, using fairness and focus. Your feedback will be far more effective, and the Receiver will probably appreciate your honesty.
- Share the good stuff, often and freely and for its own sake. Don't tuck it away in the cupboard only to be used to surround something that's much less appealing.

One of my coaching clients was an emerging leader at a television station. Micah was a top performer who was new to his leadership role, and his organization was investing in him through a series of executive coaching sessions. Moving from peer to leader, Micah was eager to learn, and one of his goals was to develop his leadership and feedback style. We began this work with a self-assessment about how he liked to give and get feedback in the workplace. Pondering this, Micah shared that he really didn't like to be recognized "publicly," and that he probably wouldn't do that with his new staff. When we dug underneath that, he shared his "aha" moment about public feedback. It turns out that a previous boss had been very effusive about praising employees in the station in the daily huddles and in the hallways. "What's wrong with that?" I inquired. Public recognition is such a healthy workplace thing! The shout-outs, the team kudos, the reinforcement is a good thing, right? Micah explained that while he was often the subject of this public praise, it always felt like it was a passive-aggressive poke at someone else who might not be measuring up. The boss always ended the praise with something snarky like "The rest of you could learn a lot from this guy." After a few of those awkward scenes, the last thing Micah wanted was to be publicly recognized by the boss. Who wants to be held up as the measuring stick to their peers, or come off as the teacher's pet? Keep praise pure. Use it for good, not as a bludgeon for bystanders.

Laura

HIGHER FREQUENCY = HIGHER LEARNING

The more frequently we check in, address questions, share a reflection, or explore an idea with the people we're working with, the more we all learn. It's unlikely that we're even aware of the subtle progress we're making together, the relationships we're forming, the understanding we're building, one connection at a time.

> A clinical study with school-aged children[2] found that they learned more effectively and performed better when given feedback before and during a learning process, rather than at the end. This seemed to allow them space to reflect and share their own learning and thoughts about the gaps between what they knew and what they didn't know as they absorbed the material. They felt autonomy and control during the process. Adults learn in much the same way.

Two words of caution here: One, don't let your routine begin to look like you're checking a box, leaving your people thinking, *"Here she comes again, same time, same place, crossing us off her list."* Shake it up, make it informal and authentic. Two, be careful not to wander into micromanagement territory, or they'll be saying to themselves, *"Once again, he's leaning over my shoulder, telling me how to do my job."* Connections should come in the form of "How's it going?" and "Where can I support you?" while avoiding a strong evaluative or instructive flavor.

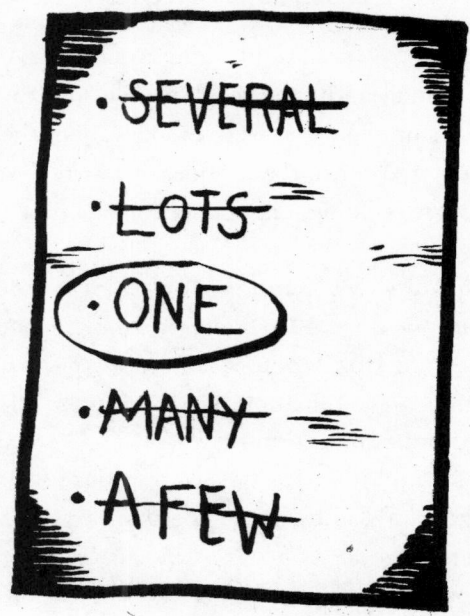

BITE-SIZE IS THE RIGHT SIZE

When you're in Extender mode, remember to keep feedback focused on bite-size bits of information. What is one suggestion, one possibility, one goal the Receiver can consider and focus on?

Why just one bite? Feedback competes with the other million bits of nonstop stimulus bombarding us constantly in the modern world and workplace. Our brains suck up information like a vacuum cleaner, and it all spins around in the canister (i.e., our short-term memory) until it is processed and either chucked out or sent to long-term memory for storage. Of course, our brains are much more sophisticated than that, but the point is that they can only handle so much information at once. Research varies, but most confirms that the human brain can only effectively process three to seven items at once. You can test this with the three-second rule. Listen to someone talk and see what you can repeat. It's unlikely you can repeat more than three seconds of content. That's all most human brains can recall at one time.

Our processing capacity is reduced even further when we're stressed. If we've triggered anxiety and fear while we're extending, then the Receiver's capacity is even more limited. Professor Amy Edmondson of the Harvard Business School suggests that fear is one of the biggest capacity killers at work, noting, "When people are interpersonally afraid, they have capacity issues. . . ."[3]

As Extenders, we have the power to help the Receiver take it in and fully process what we're sharing. Keeping it bite-size is a lighter lift for us Extenders as well. Light and easy, short and bite-size: that's the name of the extending game!

FOCUS ON THE FUTURE

Many of us will struggle to make the shift from the traditional "direct and solve" style (affectionately known at my firm as "yell and tell") to a coaching and connecting style of feedback. A powerful strategy to make this shift is to encourage dialogue that creates a shared vision of success.

When you create a shared view of the Seeker/Receiver's desired future, and you truly commit to joining forces in working toward that outcome, you build trust, and possibly even a lifelong relationship. Here are a few additional recommendations to consider:

IMAGINE WHAT COULD BE. A shared vision of future expertise, skills, or behaviors is about the possibility, the dream, the vision—and these are the ideas that drive commitment, energy, and passion.

IT'S THEIR FUTURE, NOT YOUR AGENDA. When we as Extenders merely summarize our vision of the future state as "I want you to develop your skills as a Level 3 programmer," we can give the impression that we have an ulterior motive: *I've got a gap to fill; we're not finding Level 3 programmers in the market, so I've tagged you.*

STAY THE COURSE. This commitment means you'll tackle the ups and downs together. Success is a journey that's rarely free of a few setbacks.

Anchoring conversations and connections in a shared view of the future sends a strong message that your Extender energy is focused on success.

PROGRESS, NOT PUNISHMENT

There are times in this fast-paced, hero-worshipping, social media–saturated era that we forget that achieving true expertise and proven know-how takes time. No one becomes the best at anything overnight. In the context of feedback and helping each other grow, this is a truth we cannot forget. We need an approach that plans for, supports, and recognizes progress toward those longer-term visions of success. Something like this:

BREAK IT DOWN. As an Extender, you often find yourself in a coaching role. Embrace it and help those around you consider what progress would look like against their longer-term aspirations. For example, ask a simple question like, "What steps are needed to get you there?" Once you've agreed to those steps, then make a habit of noticing how they're doing against their planned progress.

RECOGNIZE FORWARD MOTION. When progress is successfully demonstrated, take time to discuss what you noticed about their progress, all the while remembering to celebrate. Recognizing progress is a powerful motivator for more growth, and it helps keep us all in a growth mind frame.

REFRAME. If they've gone off track—maybe their behaviors or actions are getting in their way—don't dwell on what's broken and how to "fix" them as a person. Steer the conversation toward contrasting what's happening now and what needs to happen to get them where they want to be (current state versus aspirational state). Explore improvement or change without leaving the individual with the sense that they're being judged or punished.

JUST THE FACTS, MA'AM

Descriptive, data-rich, neutral, and direct feedback informs and enlightens us.

> In a study of more than 19,000 employees, the strongest lever of increased performance was found to be the "fairness and accuracy of a manager's descriptive feedback, observing direct reports and describing specific examples of what they saw or experienced, without evaluating it."[4]

Here are some pointers to take to heart as you practice your new extending style.

SHARE THE FACTS. For feedback to be fair, we need it to be descriptive, true, and grounded in relevant fact. As you're preparing to extend feedback, be sure you've noticed and gathered real information, not assumptions. If you're unsure, ask yourself:

» Is it true? How do I know?
» Do I have an example or illustration that helps me convey the facts?
» Is the observation I'm sharing my own? Is it relevant?

KEEP IT NEUTRAL. Keeping the tone neutral doesn't equate to being either a marshmallow or an emotionless robot. Neutral means factual and descriptive feedback that's free from evaluation, assessment, or judgment statements about the Receiver. When Luke asks you for feedback on how he communicated with others in the group meeting yesterday, and you tell him that he was overbearing and that he sucked the air out of the room, then, yes, you've given him some detailed noticing, but you've also embedded a judgment and a label. When we label or judge, we trip the fear switch and the connection shuts down. By judging and labeling Luke, you've assumed the power, and he's likely to be too caught up in defense mode to hear much of the conversation after that.

> *If you are still working for an organization that requires you to assign ratings and rankings to people, then my advice is to not emphasize that stuff; it's just another form of judgment and labeling. We are human beings, not numbers. Talk about the skill, the demonstrated competency. Talk about the effect their behavior is having on others and minimize the negative influence of the label.*

NO GRIT. Just the facts means dropping the gossip, rumor, innuendo, and triangulation. These behaviors bust trust and credibility. Make sure the feedback you share is directly observed by you, that it's anchored in facts, and that it's rich in helpful details. Statements that begin with "People are saying . . ." "Word around the office is . . ." or "A little mouse told me . . ." will inevitably breed paranoia and resentment. And how unfair is it to let yourself off the hook by pretending to be the innocent messenger?

SHARE EFFECTS AND EXAMPLES. Extending relevant and timely feedback should entail sharing the effects or impacts of the behavior. This adds to context and helps the Receiver understand the relevance of their actions and where to focus in the future. Did you notice something great? Share your thoughts and feelings along with the effect their actions have had. Did that process improvement your frontline employee suggested lead to a great customer satisfaction score? Don't just give them a verbal slap on the back like "Nice job on that process improvement idea." Go one step further and share the positive effect their contribution has had on your enterprise. The more we can help people connect the dots between the feedback they get about the work they do on a daily basis and how it impacts other parts or people of the organization, the stronger their emotional commitment, resilience, and willingness to change will be.

Back to Luke: If you observed another attendee shutting down during the meeting in question as Luke continued to talk, then simply share that observation, not your assessment of Luke that's based on that observation. Present the effects of his performance as you observed them and allow Luke to connect the dots and be an active participant in finding solutions that will make him a more effective contributor to the next meeting.

It's also worth noting that sharing the effects on a more personal and human level is likely to trigger the Receiver's motivation to take in and act on your noticing. For example, in a study cited by Adam Grant, organizational psychologist and *New York Times* best-selling author of *Give and Take: Why Helping Others Drives Our Success*, radiologists were assessed on the accuracy of interpreting scans. The study found that when a picture of the patient was presented alongside their corresponding X-ray, the diagnostic accuracy went up by 43 percent. Grant said, "You now know you're not just sort of looking for a fracture, you are trying to help a living breathing human being."

I'M ~~RIGHT~~, YOU'RE ~~RIGHT~~, WE'RE ALL HUMAN

Because the human brain is bombarded with information, it's evolved to take shortcuts in making choices. For example, we default to sorting people into our own mental piles: competent and incompetent, worthy and unworthy, trustworthy or suspect. Unfortunately, this very human tendency to categorize can lead us to make snap judgments about a person or group without even realizing it. As Extenders dedicated to a movement founded on fairness, we have a duty to acknowledge and challenge these biases that influence our thinking.

How do you begin taking stock of your own biases?

- Take the Implicit Association Test (IAT), created by researchers from the University of Washington, Harvard University, and the University of Virginia.[5] This test measures the strength of the links you make between concepts like race or sexuality, and how you evaluate stereotypes. It can be very enlightening.
- Choose your timing for feedback carefully. If you're feeling tired, rushed, or stressed, your biases are more likely to come into play.
- Check your facts and assumptions. Use the Fine Art of Noticing, and describe actions, intentions, and impacts clearly. Ask yourself, do I know this to be true, or am I making an assumption about this person?
- Expose yourself to ideas, images, and words that challenge any stereotypes you might hold.

Make no mistake, discriminatory and biased feedback breaks trust and can breed depression, disengagement, and a toxic environment. These outcomes alone are reason enough for me to implore leaders, managers, and peer Extenders of feedback to actively work to root out assumptions and judgment in their feedback conversations, while embracing greater inclusivity and diversity.

THEY'RE NOT LOVING WHAT YOU'RE SAYING?

I'm betting we've all experienced one of those moments when, in the midst of sharing feedback, it becomes evident that the Receiver isn't comfortable with your message. When you find yourself in that situation, don't pretend you're blind to this response. Instead, consider these options:

PRESS PAUSE. When someone objects to feedback you're offering, even if you haven't finished "delivering" it, then it's time to pump the brakes. Chances are that fear and anxiety have sideswiped the Receiver, so rambling on is not going to help. "Just let me finish" is a statement you don't want to deploy at this point. If you're standing, walk slowly to the other side of the room. If sitting, scribble in your notepad or take a sip of water. 4-7-8 breathing helps here. It may only be a brief pause, but those few seconds can allow both of you to work toward collecting yourselves.

ACKNOWLEDGE. You don't have to agree with any skeptical or dismissive remarks, and you don't have to retract your feedback if you feel it's fair and accurate, but you should acknowledge the concern shared by the Receiver. Empathy comes into play here. Say something like "I understand why you might feel that way," or "I see how that might be something you're concerned about."

REFRAME THE OBJECTION AND ASK CATALYZING QUESTIONS. Try framing the objection into a question and let the conversation flow from there. Above all, let go of the need to be right. For example, if the Receiver says, "I'm not crazy about the way you showed up during that project, either," reframe that as a question for her: "Can you help me connect my behavior to what we are talking about here?"

ASK TO HEAR MORE. When someone immediately reacts negatively to feedback, chances are that they need more information to understand what you're trying to communicate. You may also need more information in order to see their point of view, so ask for it. Try, "Could you tell me more about the problems you see with our working together?" or "When you say you weren't supported during the project, can you explain specifically how and when you felt let down?" Typically, this opens up the dialogue, allowing you to move the conversation forward and on to what to do about the feedback, and how to position the Receiver for future success. For example, you might reply to their responses with something like "Okay, now that I see what you're going through, let's take another pass at this so we can find the best solution forward for both of us."

HIT RESET. If the Receiver is clearly appeasing you by waving the white flag of surrender with statements like "Okay, whatever you say," or "Fine. I'll do it your way," then allow them a cooling-off period to formulate a more authentic response. Tell them that no firm decisions need to be made immediately, then make a plan to revisit the conversation in a couple of days. (If the issue is too pressing to wait a couple of days, then you've probably waited too long to have the conversation in the first place!)

DON'T LET THEM STEW. When connecting with a Receiver who chooses the option of going silent and stewing in their displeasure, a good prompting question is simply: "Will you tell me what you're thinking?" This gives the Receiver the power to move the conversation in whatever direction they choose (ideally, a positive direction). If their heels are still dug in, I'd suggest going back to the top of the list, pressing pause, and giving them time to prepare for a more productive conversation, whether that's a few minutes or a day.

MAKE A PLAN

Have you picked up the theme throughout this chapter that success in the Extender role is about letting go of old ideas and habits and forming new ones? Hmm, that sounds to me like a change. And every successful change needs a plan. As you set your course as an Extender, ponder these five questions:

- How can I increase my connection quotient?
- Where will I start?
- Do I need to hit reset with anyone?
- What commitments am I making to myself and others?
- What shifts do I need to embrace (i.e., old habits to quit and new ones to ingrain)? If I'm not sure, who can tell me?

Write it down, reflect often, update it as you go, and be kind to yourself as you learn and grow. Finally, make it your mission to demonstrate to the world, starting with those around you, the power of extending focused feedback that's frequent and fair, light and easy, and that celebrates progress toward a better future.

CHAPTER 9

FEEDBACK SCENARIOS FOR THE REAL WORLD

This chapter is inspired by those generous colleagues and peers who shared their feedback stories and the impact their experiences have had on their careers, their relationships, and their lives. As part of our process, they gave us—*wait for it*—feedback on the approach we should take in writing the book. "Make it real!" they said. "All of this is so helpful, but can you really show us what to do and say when things get complicated? We'd love some real-life examples that can help us apply this thinking."

They asked, and we listened. Their stories inspired the following scenarios. Try them on, adjust for fit, and incorporate them into your personal feedback movement!

Laura

SEEKERS MAKE IT REAL: SEEKER SUCCESS!

You're working hard and getting "good marks" at your current job. What you're not getting much of is feedback. There's no formal career ladder or development plan in place, but you have a great manager and you're learning a lot on the job. You're interested in taking the next step and seeking some insights about where you should focus your energy in order to advance. Here's what an excellent Seeker experience might look like when we're all leaning into our new definition of feedback.

Ask for Noticing

You focus your ask with your boss and decide against a generic prompt like "How do you think I'm doing?" Instead, you opt for a detailed, specific one: "What do you see in my work or behavior that I don't see?" This asking helps your boss know that it's okay to give you the tough stuff, and hopefully helps you identify areas you may be blind to.

Your boss takes the challenge, and his feedback is bold and honest: "I'm concerned that you don't see how you come across sometimes. It seems to me that your focus on results is so intense that you forget to acknowledge the others who helped get the work done." Wow. This hurts. But you take a deep breath and tell yourself, *I'm okay, I can handle this.* You ask, "Can you share with me one example of when I did this so I can learn more?"

Make a Plan

You and your boss collaborate and decide to create your personal "board of Extenders." You pick a couple of folks in your network whom you feel you can learn from. One is Carol, a colleague whose interaction style and work ethic you admire; the other is Jane. You've chosen to venture out of your comfort zone by enlisting Jane, since you and she often don't see eye to eye. You're pretty sure she's heavily impacted by the behavior your boss is calling out, and you see this as an opportunity to reset your relationship with Jane. This is a super-Seeker move on your part, because having a diverse board made up of both fans and critics can help you tackle the problem and truly gain perspective. It's also growth-minded of you to think, "I can learn something from anyone—even Jane!"

Go to Your Board of Extenders

Put your plan into action by seeking insights from those you've identified:

- **Admired colleague.** You set up a lunch and let Carol know that you're committed to getting better at what you do, and that you've chosen her as a mentor who can share insights to further that ambition. You let her know that, even though she's not a manager, you've noted her exceptional team-building skills. She thanks you for the feedback. (Score! You are now an Extender.) Carol gives you her perspective on what she finds works well and what is challenging for her when working on teams in the unit. You end with an agreement that she'll give you a little coaching over the next few months, then you make a plan to get back together the following week.

- **The critic.** You ask Jane for some time to walk and talk the following week. She's all about fitness, and taking a walk during a break makes it feel a little lighter than a heavy sit-down conversation. You let Jane know that you're trying to get better at working within a team, and you apologize for acting in a way that may not have reflected that lately. You tell her, "I'm curious how you are feeling about our interactions in the team meetings, specifically if there are things I'm doing (or not) that seem unfair to you." Jane says she'll think about it and she agrees to meet again.

Work Your Plan

You're off and running. You've got insights from Carol that you are testing. You have a follow-up connection scheduled with Jane, and you're open to whatever she might share. You've looped back to your boss with a quick update and a reminder about further noticing he might share. It's beginning to feel more natural working with your teammates, and you are taking the time to reflect on what's working and how it can help you grow in other ways. The real win will come a few months down the road, when Jane invites you to take a walk and asks you to mentor her on how this "Seeker" thing works!

RECEIVERS MAKE IT REAL: AVOIDING THE FREEZE AND APPEASE

It's time for the weekly walk-through of your blog content with the peer review board. You take great pride in your creativity, so the group's feedback is frequently hard for you to take in with grace.

As you leave this week's review, your publisher mentions that she's noticed you "cave in" too quickly during the feedback and editing process. She worries that your ideas are being shortchanged, leading you to rework content in ways that may not reflect your viewpoint.

You take this feedback to heart and reflect on your past experiences. You agree that you've clammed up when the senior editor pushed on key ideas. Recently, you allowed a big piece to be cut that was important to you, just because the discussion was uncomfortable. After giving it some thought and testing the feedback with a few trusted peers, you're ready to try a different approach in the weekly walk-through. You want the next session to be less of a struggle, so you commit to listening and challenging without defensiveness.

Envision the Future

This work is your portfolio. You know the kind of writer you want to be, and the nature of the content that is important to you today and for your future. You've taken the time to get clear on which ideas you're willing to go to the mat for, and which ones you're willing to let go of. This clarity empowers you as you prepare for the weekly walk-through.

Make Your Plan

Good on you for knowing that the editor's brass-tacks style tends to send you into emotional retreat, and for understanding that, while you're not able to control him, you can control your reaction to his communication style. You've also realized that your "clam up and cave in" response is not optimal, since it bogs you down in a fixed mindset. Fueled with this insight, you make your plan for the meeting by considering what techniques will help you listen and keep your cool. Maybe you take notes on two sides of a sheet of paper you've prepared—one half for those ideas that are being challenged but that you want to keep, the other side for those you're willing to let go of. You plan your go-to quick physical rescue technique: take one big deep breath, exhale slowly, and say to yourself, I can listen and choose.

Manage in the Moment

When you find yourself wanting to defend during the peer review, you suspend the thought for a moment and instead contemplate what you're hearing in light of those ideas you've identified as important enough to advocate for. At one point, the rapid flow of conversation leaves you in its wake, so you say, "Let's back up and talk a little more about that for a minute." You state your case calmly and without judgment, then ask for clarity: "I can understand why you want to scrap the piece on climate change. However,

I feel differently. My view is this section is one of the key issues in this edition, so changing this alters the whole tone of the piece. How committed are you to this change?" With this question, you have invited disagreement and shown that you are willing to discuss, not just defend. This propels the conversation and allows you to find a solution that holds true to your values while incorporating feedback that will make the piece stronger.

RECEIVERS MAKE IT REAL: THE TOUGHEST (AND BEST) RECEIVING YOU'LL EVER DO

You're up for promotion from a mid-level position in a nonprofit to managing director of a new division. You've overseen several administrative areas, including finance, human resources, and curriculum and instruction. You've enjoyed steady progress in your career and believe you're the right candidate. You've worked closely with the chief executive officer and the chief financial officer, and you know Nalu, the other leading candidate, well. His career track has been similar to yours, though he's spent half as many years at this organization as you have. If you get the job, Nalu will work for you. He's a great worker and respected by his people, but he has a reputation for being brutally frank.

You don't get the job. You feel strongly that you should have, and you feel angry and humiliated. You flee the building and call Nalu on the way home to "congratulate" him. Your primitive mind is at the wheel, so you say, "Hey, Nalu. Congrats. I, uh, don't really know what happened because I feel pretty strongly that I should have the job. But that's fine. Anyway, well done." Nalu, in his typically blunt style, responds with the most powerful and painful feedback you've ever received: "Actually, you should not have this job. Know why? You're arrogant. Look, you have a lot of strengths. You have a reputation for hitting your numbers, you know the organization, you can paint a great vision and lay out a powerful strategy, but you're disconnected from your people and they don't enjoy working for you. I'm honored to have this job, and I honor and value the people who work for me. That's why I got the job and you didn't."

Don't Rush to React

Your initial reaction is pure fury. Wisely, knowing you're not in a good place, you give yourself the weekend to take this all in. On Saturday morning, you go for a long walk and decide you need to get your head together. You decide the first step is to put what you're feeling into words. You muster the courage to honestly acknowledge your emotions in writing: *I feel blindsided. I feel hurt. I'm uncertain of where I stand, which is scary.* You also take time to do some much-needed self-affirmation, reflecting on the idea that the positive aspects of your identity that Nalu recognized are as much a part of your story as the negative ones he confronted you with. This self-recognition lessens the physical response to threat, and helps you become more open to this powerful and critical feedback. You also remind yourself that who you are in your work life represents only one facet of your identity: you're also a supportive friend, a devoted community member, and a loving spouse and parent of two teenagers. The bigger picture helps you put Nalu's feedback in its proper perspective, and you wake up Sunday morning ready to move forward. You call Nalu that evening to apologize and extend your sincere congratulations, then ask him for time to talk in the coming week.

Seek More Information

You thank Nalu for recognizing many of your strengths and for the blunt, yet painful feedback on your weak areas. Now you're in Seeker mode as you add, "The major point I'd like your insights on is about being arrogant, aloof, and disconnected from my people. I see myself as a leader of others, ideally at this organization. So, you're right: I need to improve. What are the one or two things you think I should start working on to move in a better direction?"

Epilogue: From Prove to Improve

Nalu was right, despite his imperfect delivery style. Fortunately, your newfound Receiver skills served you well as you accepted his blunt feedback, and you shifted your thinking from proving you were the better person for the job to improving your leadership skills. You chose to focus on the path forward, and now you've done the hard work necessary to change your style, aided by a year of coaching and connecting with Nalu, as well as some focused seeking from your direct reports and others. In the coming year, you'll move to a comparable leadership role at another organization, starting fresh and emerging strong. You continue to express gratitude for Nalu's deep and honest feedback, and you often relate the story of the mentor and peer who cared enough to tell it to you straight, of your strengths and your screwups, and how listening and making a choice for growth changed the trajectory of your career.

EXTENDERS MAKE IT REAL: NOTHING, NOTHING, THEN . . . BOOM!

You're the boss. One of your best project managers, Mai Ling, is in charge of a team delivering the $2 million redesign of a factory shop floor in another country. A major milestone has been missed, and you get a call from your irate client.

Mai Ling has been known to miss a deadline now and then, but all in all, she's a great performer. You know you should give feedback "in the moment," but you let it slide for now because she works in a different country and time zone. Previously, you've chosen not to address earlier milestone misses, since she's leading one of the organization's top projects, she's adored by her team, and she works harder than just about anyone. She's also one of the few remaining women in the company to earn a Six Sigma Master Black Belt project improvement methodology certification. However, the tongue-lashing you just received from the client has kicked your acute stress response into high gear, so you pick up the phone and let Mai Ling have it: "It was not fun getting my ass chewed by the client today, Mai Ling. You half-stepped the deadline and ruined our chances of winning the next bid. You've missed something like five deadlines in the past few months. What the hell is up?"

Check Your Bias

Since Mai Ling hasn't heard anything from you about missing deadlines, you've set a precedent that they're okay with you. You may be suffering from the halo effect, a bias that refers to our tendency to form a generalized positive impression of another based on a single attribute or event (in this case, the attribute is Mai Ling's coveted Master Black Belt certification).

Increase Frequency

Practicing the Fine Act of Noticing and checking in more frequently with Mai Ling will let her know that you place a high priority on her work and are there to support her through good times and bad.

Check Your Intent

Ask yourself who this feedback is really about. You're worked up because the client screamed at you, and it was embarrassing to be caught unaware. But before delivering feedback, think carefully about what your message should be. Is your intention to help Mai Ling learn and grow? Then make yourself heard. If it's simply to vent, then bite your tongue.

Don't Shame or Blame

"You half-stepped the deadline" is a judgmental statement. It's better to mine for the facts ("Why was the deadline missed?"), describe the impact fairly ("This could mean losing work from this client next year"), and then, using whatever techniques help you remain calm, extend the conversation to seek ways to avert future problems. You might say, "I know we both want to deliver this project on time and on budget. Can you break down last week's events and let me work with you to avoid a repeat of these issues?"

Help Mai Ling Imagine the Future

Reinforce your confidence in Mai Ling. Rather than demanding changes in her behavior or her process, help her envision how a great track record for delivering on time could drive her career growth by asking, "What steps are necessary to enhance your reputation as a consistent on-time producer in the future?" This approach should produce intrinsic motivation, which is far more likely to lead to rapid and lasting change.

EXTENDERS MAKE IT REAL: THERE'S SOMETHING ABOUT MARY

Mary has been known to be late for the weekly Monday morning stand-up. She also has a reputation as an avid social drinker outside the office, so you suspect that's a contributing factor. Mary shows up late for the third time in a row on a Monday morning and misses the first 15 minutes of the stand-up. It feels like she is disrespecting you and the rest of her team, intentionally skipping these mandatory meetings. You tell her you need to talk to her about her drinking and how it's not acceptable to slide in at nine a.m.

You meet with Mary behind closed doors, and as she settles into a chair across from you at your desk, you can see that her coworkers have begun to take notice of your meeting. You begin by chastising her for her tardiness, and when you mention your suspicions about her drinking, she begins to cry. She reveals that she's recently begun taking her stepson to therapy sessions across town on Monday mornings, and that getting him to school and then making it to the office in time for the stand-up is impossible. She says that this is something she hadn't felt comfortable discussing with you previously because it was a private family matter.

Connect First

There is real opportunity for empathy and connection here. Mary works with you daily, yet you didn't know (until now) that she even has a stepson. It's clearly time to get to know Mary, so set up a lunch, and work with her on a schedule that allows her to fulfill both her personal and professional obligations.

Seek a Solution Together

Together you and Mary reach the conclusion that what is really important is her participation in the stand-up, not that the stand-up occur at nine on Mondays. You agree to poll the team to see if they can shift to a noon or three p.m. stand-up on her stepson's therapy days or set up video calls for the days when Mary or others can't make it in person.

Moderate Positional Power and Stick to the Facts

Pulling Mary into your office while the rest of the team watches may feel like a power move or punishment. Next time, ask permission to talk, suggest moving to a private location, and sit side by side while talking. Noticing the facts and extending empathy without judgment will save you from the embarrassment of not being in the know in the future, while also giving Mary the opportunity to explain the circumstances. A good opener would be: "Mary, I've noticed you've been late for the stand-up the last few Mondays. This impacts the team because we delay our start time waiting for you, and we don't get your team's updates. I'm here to help. Can you share with me what's going on?"

THE GREAT DRAMA TRIANGLE

As you're about to close the restaurant, Sol pops his head out of the kitchen door to say goodbye, then adds, "By the way, I don't think Mac appreciates the way you wrote up the schedule last week. You gave Sam two tip-heavy shifts on the restaurant floor, and Mac got stuck with hosting duties." Sol tells you that Mac even went so far as to say that you're the worst manager he's ever dealt with.

Shut Down the Triangle

Start by asking Sol if he'd directed Mac to come directly to you when he was sharing this information—something like, "I'm curious if you asked Mac to come to me directly with that feedback?" If he didn't, let Sol know that if he receives feedback like this again, you'd appreciate it if he'd encourage the person to come directly to you. Be straight about the behaviors you value by saying, "I really like to communicate in person with my team and talking about the schedule without me isn't helpful because I can't change it."

If Sol tells you that Mac is too intimidated to speak to you directly, you might enlist Sol to be a third-party "coach" who could meet with you and Mac. Either way, let Sol know that you appreciate the insights, and that you'll follow up directly with Mac. Assure Sol that you don't intend to throw him under the proverbial bus, and that you'll approach the conversation with Mac wanting to understand more about how you can work better with him.

Approach without Judgment

Let Mac know that you'd like to find a time when the two of you can discuss the scheduling. When you get together, start the conversation by sharing that you've heard about his frustrations. Ask him to share more about the impact your scheduling approach is having on him directly. Once you've taken his views in and talked about solutions together, close the conversation by noting that you'll expect him to come directly to you with any concerns in the future.

Solutions for Sol

For Sol, the third party in the triangle, there are constructive ways for him to extract himself from the uncomfortable middle. As Mac shared his initial anger over the schedule with him, Sol might have said, "What did the boss say about this issue? Have you had that discussion?" If Mac said he hadn't mentioned it, then Sol might suggest that doing so could lead to a solution.

If Mac continues to triangulate, Sol should ask him if he's just venting, or if Mac expects Sol to take some kind of action. If it's the former, Sol should let him get it off his chest, leave the words there in the room, and encourage Mac to talk to the boss. If Mac expects Sol to do something, Sol should seek clarity about what that is. He could offer to help coach Mac on how to approach you while politely declining to deliver the message for him.

You're the Boss

If this isn't the first time that triangulation of this nature has happened within your team, you might be realizing that you have a bigger problem. Maybe this behavior has become the norm and it's time to address it head-on. If this is the case, use CONNECT to engage your team in the conversation, and as a tool they can use to bust old habits.

CHAPTER 10

IMAGINE

WE'VE SHARED OUR COLLECTIVE experiences, advanced our thinking with compelling research, refined and enhanced our ideas, boiled it down, and bared all with the intention of helping you do good work and be your best self. We've made the case for our movement, explored the science behind it, and offered tangible tactics and models for a new brand of feedback—feedback that helps us thrive, improve, and grow while reducing the pain and resentment that too often results from old-school thinking and misguided practices. We've shown you how you can engage as a Seeker, a Receiver, and an Extender. We've given you tips, tricks, models, and guidelines. But now that we've laid it all out, we've got a confession to make: There's something bigger going on here. Something bigger than just you.

Set aside today's reality and dream with me for a moment. Imagine the impact we will have when we put our collective efforts into redefining feedback. Imagine the results when our shared energy is directed toward creating work environments fueled by positive connections. Imagine creating cultures in which feedback flourishes and our proven practices of seeking, receiving, and extending feedback are the accepted norm. Imagine a world where we feel safe being authentic and transparent about who we are, and just as open about the work we still need to do to be who we want to be. A world where we let go of the fear and embrace the help others offer us, and where our energy, time, and momentum are always oriented toward the future. Imagine.

We want to live in that world! We want it for our organization, for your organization, and for all the teams of people out there working to cure cancer, create new sources of energy, heal the sick, pave roads, cut hair, grill hamburgers, dream up new flavors of ice cream, and all the other things that make life worth living. It's the experience we want our children to have as they enter the workplace, and our parents to have as they bid it a gradual farewell.

Clients often assure us that they want to build a culture of feedback for their people. But we are not so sure that they're imagining it in the same way that we are. Do they really understand that we're not just talking about turning up the volume on the old ideas and approaches? Do they understand that we are not merely advocating for putting our energy into more timely or complete review forms? Are they ready and willing to let go of control, labels, and centralized power?

So, as we wrap up, we want to remind you that our new version of feedback is defined as having *the sole intention of helping*. The movement will be led by Seekers, supported by thoughtful Extenders, and encouraged by open Receivers. It will flow across teams and people in a manner that is easy, genuine, and informal. It will feel new, and it will take us some time to get comfortable with it. It won't be a linear path. It will succeed if and when we individually and collectively show up differently.

As our parting gift, we present some easy practices that your team can use to build feedback muscles and learn together. These ideas offer an easy starting place to open the door to opportunities for team and peer feedback. They provide a great way to practice feedback as we've defined it for our new world. Try them on, tweak them to fit, create some of your own, and let them help you move your team forward.

- End every meeting with an exercise that allows the attendees to reflect on the goodness of the meeting or the topic at hand. At PeopleFirm we call it "Bs & Cs" (benefits and concerns). One of my clients does "liked it, learned it, lacked it." Or you can always fall back to the old tried and true plus/minus.
- Devote a few minutes during team meetings to expressing gratitude. Ask for the group to call out a "thank you" to others. Don't force it, but encourage sharing.
- Launch a simple peer feedback process. It doesn't have to be heavy; simple and light is best. "Feedback Fridays" are a fun way to start building muscle one day at a time.
- Welcome employees into talent reviews to share their aspirations and development wishes. At PeopleFirm we like to say, "Nothing about me without me." Giving employees this opportunity to be direct recipients of feedback about their careers is a powerful means of reinforcing the principle that they need to lead the way in determining their own growth and advancement.

These ideas should help you get started. Marry them with the practices we've shared throughout this book. Just remember to keep it frequent and light; rich in gratitude, recognition, and positive feedback; and clear, factual, and bite-size. Focus all that on future growth and we'll be well on our way to creating a world where feedback is no longer a dirty word.

NOTES

CHAPTER 1

1. Marcus Buckingham, "Most HR Data Is Bad Data," *Harvard Business Review*, February 9, 2015, https://hbr.org/2015/02/most-hr-data-is-bad-data.
2. Office Vibe, "The Global State of Employee Engagement," https://www.officevibe.com/state-employee-engagement.

CHAPTER 2

1. Gerry Ledford, "Performance Feedback Culture Drives Business Impact," i4cp, June 21, 2018, https://www.i4cp.com/productivity-blog/performance-feedback-culture-drives-business-impact.
2. Gretchen Spreitzer and Christine Porath, "Creating Sustainable Performance," *Harvard Business Review*, January-February 2012, https://hbr.org/2012/01/creating-sustainable-performance.
3. Joseph Folkman, "The Best Gift Leaders Can Give: Honest Feedback," *Forbes*, December 19, 2013, https://www.forbes.com/sites/joefolkman/2013/12/19/the-best-gift-leaders-can-give-honest-feedback/.
4. Joseph Folkman, "Top Ranked Leaders Know This Secret: Ask for Feedback," *Forbes*, January 8, 2015, https://www.forbes.com/sites/joefolkman/2015/01/08/top-ranked-leaders-know-this-secret-ask-for-feedback/.

CHAPTER 3

1. Shirzad Chamine, *Positive Intelligence* (Austin, TX: Greenleaf Book Group, 2012).

2. Roy Baumeister, Ellen Bratslavsky, Kathleen Vohs, and Catrin Finkenauer, "Bad Is Stronger than Good," *Review of General Psychology* 5, no. 4 (2001): 323–370.

3. Carol S. Dweck, *Mindset: The New Psychology of Success* (New York: Ballantine Books, 2008).

4. C. S. Dweck and E. L. Leggett, "A Social-Cognitive Approach to Motivation and Personality," *Psychological Review* 95, no. 2 (1988): 256–273, https://www.mindsetworks.com/Science/Impact.

CHAPTER 5

1. John Gottman, general study findings, https://www.gottman.com/about /research/.

2. Kyle Benson, "The Magic Relationship Ratio, According to Science," Gottman Institute, October 4, 2017, https://www.gottman.com/blog/the-magic -relationship-ratio-according-science/.

3. Corporate Leadership Council, 2002, "Building the High-Performance Workforce: A Quantitative Analysis of the Effectiveness of Performance Management Strategies. Corporate Executive Board," https://docplayer.net /5496089-Building-the-high-performance-workforce-a-quantitative -analysis-of-the-effectiveness-of-performance-management-strategies.html.

4. Ben Yagoda, "The Cognitive Biases Tricking Your Brain," *Atlantic*, September 2018, https://www.theatlantic.com/magazine/archive/2018 /09/cognitive-bias/565775/.

CHAPTER 6

1. Gerry Ledford, "Performance Feedback Culture Drives Business Impact," i4cp, June 21, 2018, https://www.i4cp.com/productivity-blog/performance -feedback-culture-drives-business-impact.

2. 2018 SHRM/Globoforce Employee Recognition Survey, https://resources
.globoforce.com/home/findings-from-the-2018-shrm-globoforce
-employee-recognition-survey-designing-work-cultures-for-the-human
-era.

CHAPTER 7

1. Sonja Lyubomirsky, Kristin Layous, Joseph Chancellor, and S. Katherine
Nelson, "Thinking About Rumination: The Scholarly Contributions and
Intellectual Legacy of Susan Nolen-Hoeksema," *Annual Review of Clinical Psychology* 11 (March 2015): 1–22, https://doi.org/10.1146/annurev-clinpsy
-032814-112733.

CHAPTER 8

1. Jack Zenger, "The Vital Role of Positive Feedback as a Leadership Strength,"
Forbes, May 5, 2017, https://www.forbes.com/sites/jackzenger/2017/07/05
/the-vital-role-of-positive-feedback-as-a-leadership-strength.

2. Elizabeth Marsh, Lisa Fazio, and Anna Goswick, "Memorial Consequences of Testing School-Aged Children," August 15, 2013, https://www
.ncbi.nlm.nih.gov/pmc/articles/PMC3700528/.

3. Amy Edmondson, "Psychological Safety and Learning Behavior in Work
Teams," *Administrative Science Quarterly* 44, no. 2 (1999): 350–383, https://
doi.org/10.2307/2666999.

4. Corporate Leadership Council, "Building the High-Performance Workforce."

5. "Who Created the IAT?" http://www.understandingprejudice.org/iat/faq
.htm.

ACKNOWLEDGMENTS

THEY SAY IT TAKES a village, but we say it takes a tribe. We couldn't have written this book without ours.

THE BOOK TRIBE

JENNI CLARK: Thank you for your care and your loyalty to us and to this project. Your ability to juggle multiple and massive work streams, artists, and authors with a joyful and uplifting spirit made this project not only possible but also enjoyable. We adore you.

JEFF MOSIER: Our editor, muse, and champion of straight talk. This book, like the last, would not be what it is without your hard work, dedication, and patience. Your ability to speak to and through us is a true gift. Additionally, thank you for continuing to be Tamra's superpower. We should all be so lucky.

TODD VICIAN: Our thanks to PeopleFirm's "Chief People Dude" and content reviewer extraordinaire for thoughtfully examining every word, adding your insights, and always guiding us in directions none of the rest of us had even considered.

THE PEOPLEFIRM LEADERSHIP SOLUTIONS TEAM of Bill Hefferman, Bill Harrison, Michelle Fanfarillo, and Roger Kastner: Your focused feedback, coaching, and contributions to the content of this book have made it so much better than it otherwise would have been.

THE ART TRIBE

Much love and gratitude to our "in-house" design team, Ivy Chandler Mosier and Logan Grealish, who were busy working multiple other jobs (Ivy) and finishing a degree at UW (Logan) when our plea to "mock up a few quick images" came in. Your creativity has contributed so much to the irreverent and unconventional nature of this book. We are lucky to have had the joy of both giving birth to and working with such talented and caring humans.

THE PEOPLEFIRM TRIBE

Thanks to the entire PeopleFirm tribe, who beta-tested our ideas, encouraged us, and provided us with valuable feedback throughout the process. Thank you to our beloved curmudgeon-in-chief, Alan Borgida, for his overall support, time, and space to make this investment. Thanks to Scott Perkins for standing with us and always being a champion of our work. A special shout-out to Gina Napoli, who had the courage to tell us to add another "N" so CONNECT would be spelled correctly.

THE MENTORS AND MUSES

We owe much to Seth Godin, the late Judith Glaser and Doug Silsbee, Jack Zegner and Joseph Folkman, Dr. John Gottman, and Shirzad Chamine for the profound influence their research and published works have had on our thinking.

To our clients and colleagues across the globe: Our connections with you inspired this work. We learned from you. These are your stories. Thank you for allowing us to work for you and alongside you.

THANKS TO THE PEOPLE WHO GAVE IT TO US STRAIGHT

DENNIS HARTMAN: On our weekly drive to Oberto headquarters, you told me to stop hesitating and start leading. It was the kick in the butt I needed to set me on the course that's brought me to where I am today.—Tamra

VIC MOSES: Twenty-odd years ago I was at a career pivot point. "God allows U-turns," you said, so I quit the job that was wrong for me and came back to where I could use my strengths to their fullest. Your feedback changed me, and I am forever grateful. —Laura

THE BERRETT-KOEHLER TRIBE

Neal and the rest of the great team at BK: Thanks for taking on Book #2; you are a valued and trusted partner.

We're also grateful for the thorough and thoughtful feedback we received from BK's peer reviewers, Barry, Leigh, and Joe.

AND MOST OF ALL, THE FAMILY TRIBES

The Mosier family (Jeff, Wilson, Ivy, and Al Chandler); the Grealish family (Jeff, Evann, Logan, Camden, Kevin, Caleb, and Lisa Dowling, too); the Clark family (Jonathan, Luke, and Micah); and the Vician family (Michelle, Lucas, and Carter): Thank you for feeding us, encouraging us, and bringing Laura wine when she whined. Thanks also to Perry and Luna for lying on Tamra's feet while she worked. We owe you everything for tolerating all the late-night toil, weekend working sessions, and missed walks around the lake. We'll make it up to you, we promise.

And to Big Dick and the Extenders: Thanks for the inspiration. RIP, Big Dick.

INDEX

ABOUT THE AUTHORS

Jenni Clark Photography

M. TAMRA CHANDLER

M. TAMRA CHANDLER is the founder and CEO of PeopleFirm LLC, one of *Forbes* magazine's 2018 "America's Best Management Consulting Firms." A nationally recognized thought leader, author, and speaker, Tamra has spent most of her 30-year career developing new and effective ways for people and their organizations to perform at their peak. In 2016, she wrote the acclaimed book *How Performance Management Is Killing Performance—and What to Do About It*, which has been published in three languages.

Tamra started PeopleFirm with a unique vision: to deliver measurable, meaningful results using people-centered solutions. Under her leadership, PeopleFirm has become a go-to partner for more than 125 clients, including Microsoft, Nordstrom, Alaska Airlines, Nike, WorldPay, Christiana Health Care System, and the Bill & Melinda Gates Foundation. PeopleFirm's one-of-a-kind approach is grounded in research and delivers strategic, approachable, action-oriented solutions for nearly every industry. In keeping with the company motto, "Your people = Your success," PeopleFirm consistently earns high marks from its regional and national clients, as well as recognition as one of the Pacific Northwest's top places to work.

Tamra has devoted three decades to developing new methods for building aspirational cultures, aligning leaders and teams to compelling strategies, modernizing HR, rethinking performance management, and transforming organizational models. While helping organizations across the world modernize their performance management programs, she has applied that same focus to studying and uncovering the feedback dilemma and its implications for human performance.

Tamra draws continued inspiration and support from her husband, Jeff; their young adult children, Ivy and Wilson; her father, Al; and her faithful pedigreed mutts, Perry and Luna.

LAURA DOWLING GREALISH

LAURA is a senior consultant and executive coach with PeopleFirm and has spent the past two decades studying and applying the disciplines and science that help clients create thriving environments, high-performing teams, modern performance management techniques, improved organizational effectiveness, and customized learning and development programs.

Her career experiences have allowed her to embrace a "craftsman mindset" as she gathers insights across industries and people disciplines. Before partnering with Tamra at PeopleFirm, Laura's career path included stops at organizations like GE Capital, Genworth Financial, the Cleveland Clinic, and Russell Investments.

Laura has a bachelor of arts degree in business management from the University of Montana and an MBA from Pacific Lutheran University. She and her husband, Jeff, live in the Pacific Northwest and enjoy having their two adult children, Evann and Logan, nearby, along with a growing tribe of little grandpeople.

More from M. Tamra Chandler

How Performance Management Is Killing Performance —and What to Do About It

Rethink, Redesign, Reboot

Most people associate performance management with the annual review, universally dreaded by employees, management, and HR professionals alike. It's a cookie-cutter, fear-based, top-down approach that has never motivated anyone to do anything but try to avoid it. But Tamra Chandler has a groundbreaking alternative that works.

Rooted in the latest scientific findings about motivation, Chandler's Performance Management Reboot approach is thoroughly transparent and employee driven. It celebrates collaboration over competition and rewards people for acquiring new skills and increasing their contribution instead of hitting arbitrary benchmarks. Chandler walks you through each step in creating a process that will help you meet the three objectives of great performance management: developing your people, rewarding them equitably, and driving your organization's performance.

Hardcover, 256 pages, ISBN 978-1-62656-677-4
PDF ebook, ISBN 978-1-62656-678-1
ePub ebook ISBN 978-1-62656-679-8
Digital audio, ISBN 978-1-62656-835-8

Berrett–Koehler Publishers, Inc.
www.bkconnection.com   **800.929.2929**

Berrett–Koehler Publishers

Berrett-Koehler is an independent publisher dedicated to an ambitious mission: *Connecting people and ideas to create a world that works for all.*

Our publications span many formats, including print, digital, audio, and video. We also offer online resources, training, and gatherings. And we will continue expanding our products and services to advance our mission.

We believe that the solutions to the world's problems will come from all of us, working at all levels: in our society, in our organizations, and in our own lives. Our publications and resources offer pathways to creating a more just, equitable, and sustainable society. They help people make their organizations more humane, democratic, diverse, and effective (and we don't think there's any contradiction there). And they guide people in creating positive change in their own lives and aligning their personal practices with their aspirations for a better world.

And we strive to practice what we preach through what we call "The BK Way." At the core of this approach is *stewardship,* a deep sense of responsibility to administer the company for the benefit of all of our stakeholder groups, including authors, customers, employees, investors, service providers, sales partners, and the communities and environment around us. Everything we do is built around stewardship and our other core values of *quality, partnership, inclusion,* and *sustainability.*

This is why Berrett-Koehler is the first book publishing company to be both a B Corporation (a rigorous certification) and a benefit corporation (a for-profit legal status), which together require us to adhere to the highest standards for corporate, social, and environmental performance. And it is why we have instituted many pioneering practices (which you can learn about at www.bkconnection.com), including the Berrett-Koehler Constitution, the Bill of Rights and Responsibilities for BK Authors, and our unique Author Days.

We are grateful to our readers, authors, and other friends who are supporting our mission. We ask you to share with us examples of how BK publications and resources are making a difference in your lives, organizations, and communities at www.bkconnection.com/impact.

Dear reader,

Thank you for picking up this book and welcome to the worldwide BK community! You're joining a special group of people who have come together to create positive change in their lives, organizations, and communities.

What's BK all about?

Our mission is to connect people and ideas to create a world that works for all.

Why? Our communities, organizations, and lives get bogged down by old paradigms of self-interest, exclusion, hierarchy, and privilege. But we believe that can change. That's why we seek the leading experts on these challenges—and share their actionable ideas with you.

A welcome gift

To help you get started, we'd like to offer you a **free copy** of one of our bestselling ebooks:

www.bkconnection.com/welcome

When you claim your **free ebook**, you'll also be subscribed to our blog.

Our freshest insights

Access the best new tools and ideas for leaders at all levels on our blog at ideas.bkconnection.com.

Sincerely,

Your friends at Berrett-Koehler